KICK

TAKE CONTROL OF THE

ANXIETY'S

UNCONTROLLABLE FORCE IN YOUR LIFE

ASS

KICK

TAKE CONTROL OF THE

ANXIETY'S

UNCONTROLLABLE FORCE IN YOUR LIFE

ASS

DR. BHRETT MCCABE

606 PUBLISHING

ACKNOWLEDGEMENTS

You do not write a book without the support of those around you. Thank you to Brett Basham who has been invaluable with the content guidance, design of the book, and organizational flow and vision of this project. Thank you to Dr. Kevin Alschuler for the early review and psychological perspectives to ensure that the content of the book can stand on its own merits. Thank you to my wife, Missy, for everything from living with a spouse with intense anxiety and providing unconditional support to reading every iteration of this book, even though she does not suffer from anxiety. To my wonderful daughters, Logan and Caroline, I pray that your experience with me with anxiety shows the fruits of the world can always be fulfilling by simply appreciating what you have. To my mom and late father for understanding my anxiety, never making me feel wrong for feeling what I felt, and, most importantly, for showing me that mental health counseling was a powerful path to follow. Without a few psychologists, I would have never been in this position. To Phil Brantley, you were the best trainer of psychologists. To Justin Nash, your mentorship changed me and continues to impact me profoundly. To Laura LHerrison, thank you for showing me the way many years ago. To my clients, thank you for believing in me.

Finally, I want to share this prayer that has brought me such peace in my life. You may think of it as the AA (Alcoholics Anonymous) prayer, but it is so much bigger. I hope you find it as inspiring as I do.

PRAYER FOR SERENITY

God, grant me the serenity
to accept the things I cannot change,
the courage to change the things I can,
and the wisdom to know the difference.
Living one day at a time,
enjoying one moment at a time;
accepting hardship as a pathway to peace;
taking, as Jesus did,
this sinful world as it is,
not as I would have it;
trusting that You will make all things right
if I surrender to Your will;
so that I may be reasonably happy in this life
and supremely happy with You forever in the next. Amen.

Reinhold Niebuhr

PREFACE

This book is about the influence of anxiety on your life, both your overall well-being and your performance. Throughout this book, I will flow between those two domains, sometimes with clear distinctions and other times with fluidity. The most important consideration is that anxiety is part of everything you do but does not have to destroy your progress, confidence, or resiliency.

Anxiety has become so prevalent today that it is one of the most common presenting complaints for new clients. If you do not experience anxiety, you will at some point in your life. I hate to paint that bleak picture, but you have so many demands on you that anxiety is often the only effective coping mechanism. The danger is when it interferes with your life, performance, and recovery from stress.

Before I venture into the depths of anxiety, it is vital to understand the competitive mindset and why anxiety interferes. Every competitor is looking for an edge against the competition, an advantage against the opponent, and wants to elevate their game. Driving that desire is often a realization or awareness that you can be better and that others are improving or performing better than you are. In the competitive world, that awareness drives urgency, which elevates anxiety. In the regular experience of life, the realization that life could be better, that you are falling behind others, that something could go wrong, or someone could be disappointed in you drives you to improve. Unfortunately, those same feelings elevate anxiety.

Those are the unfortunate facts. Anxiety has benefits, and then it becomes uncomfortable, unbearable, and disruptive.

I remember one of my prominent professional clients pulling me aside before a big game and telling me that he had started to experience insomnia, could not turn his mind off, and struggled to let go of mistakes. Despite playing well, he was struggling in private.

"Doc, this is new to me. I am embarrassed that what I saw as a weakness in others is now my daily struggle. I have waited a month to tell you because I thought it would just go away."

I told him I was proud of him for sharing and facing the anxiety. Most importantly, anxiety does not have to be in control of his life, his mindset, or his experience.

Finally, I said, "I want to challenge you to see anxiety as a competition. Imagine that the angst you feel is stealing a piece of you every day, and with every worry that you feel that is out of your control, you are losing a part of your edge. Would you sit there and worry that you are losing, or will you prepare to kick its ass? Will you hope you improve, or will you take control? It is time to lock in and take control.

CONTENTS

Introduction   *1*

CHAPTER 1 – SETTING THE STAGE   11

CHAPTER 2 – THE UNITED STATES OF ANXIETY,   21
DEPRESSION, AND STRESS

CHAPTER 3 – SO, ANXIETY DEVELOPS?   29

CHAPTER 4 – THE INCOMING TSUNAMI   45

CHAPTER 5 – CALLING AN AUDIBLE ON ANXIETY   57

CHAPTER 6 – YOU GOT THIS!   67

CHAPTER 7 – ENTER THE RING WITH THE MINDSET   73
OF AUTHORITY

CHAPTER 8 – GETTING RIGHT   79

CHAPTER 9 – THE POWER IN PERSPECTIVE   85

CHAPTER 10 – THE POWER OF ACCEPTANCE   91

CHAPTER 11 – STOP RUNNING FROM ANXIETY – FACE IT!   103

CHAPTER 12 – WHAT YOU FOCUS ON YOU BECOME   113

CHAPTER 13 – SUFFER POWERFULLY   123

CHAPTER 14 – BUILD A PROCESS FOR YOUR LIFE   131

CHAPTER 15 – BUILD YOUR SUPPORT   147

CHAPTER 16 – BE PATIENT   157

CHAPTER 17 – IT ALL COMES DOWN TO   165
EMOTIONAL DISCIPLINE

CHAPTER 18 – THE PATHWAY TO WINNING   179

CHAPTER 19 – ANXIETY IS NOT A LIFE SENTENCE   199

INTRODUCTION

The weather was stifling – humid and sticky with a temperature rivaling the heat emanating from the sun. With sweat running down my face, my stomach turned and flipped over like an Olympic gymnast performing for the judges on the biggest night of her career. My mind was immersed in a war of good versus evil, searching for any way to escape the pain of the moment and for any chance to run away from the long, metal cylinder that was Continental Airlines' Houston to New Orleans afternoon route.

The Taco Bell soft tacos and bean burritos were fighting to make an encore appearance as I sat in my exit row seat, waiting for the airplane to push back from the gate. I was sitting next to one of my graduate school colleagues, and I was not going to embarrass myself. No way would I vomit on this plane—zero freaking chance.

My stomach was increasingly unsettled, my mind raced, my heart pounded, and my arms dripped in sweat. I could taste that overly sweet taste of pre-vomit saliva. I wouldn't say I like vomit – yours or mine. It may be the feeling of losing control or the experience of your insides rushing to find the nearest opening. I'm not sure what it is, but I hate it.

My colleague could not know what was happening. He was my chief intern, and I looked up to him.

"Only a loser would puke right now!"

"I was an athlete; fight this!"

"I just want to be home. My God, please help me right now!"

It was the longest 20 minutes of my life as anxiety took me down a dark, painful road. I tried to refocus on surviving the misery of this moment, but I was overwhelmed by negativity, fear, and shame. I was soaked in sweat as if sitting in a sinking canoe in a thunderstorm. I was trying to keep my vomit down and make it home.

It was a harrowing experience. I had never felt anything of that intensity before, and I remember thinking that dying in a plane crash would be a relief—weird, morbid thinking on full display.

My name is Bhrett McCabe, and I suffer from anxiety.

March 13, 2000. I suffered my first panic attack. I was twenty-seven years old, and my life changed immediately.

I have always been anxious. I don't know why. Just who I am.

The Gurgle Started Early in My Life

My struggle with anxiety goes way back. I wish I could identify my early experiences with anxiety to one horrendous moment, but it has always been there for me. I remember riding to school in the 5th grade, the best year of my school life ever, and worrying about how the day would go, what could happen, and whether things would be okay. It seemed that every day, passing the same house on the school route, I had a stomachache that felt like an emergency visit to a toilet was necessary, yet as soon as I walked into the school, it would go away.

I chewed my fingernails like I had dipped them in candy. I tried the bitter nail polish, but that did not stop me. I bit my fingernails because anxiety ate me up from the inside, not because I enjoyed biting my fingernails. I had to relieve my stress, and I needed relief.

The only place I felt normal was on the baseball field. I had zero anxiety on the diamond until high school, but that was more related to wanting to perform well and not worrying about letting people down or embarrassing myself. I was shy, quiet, and a loner for a long time in high school. I never really thought I was anxious then, but writing this now, I was then, too.

I did not vomit on that airplane. It was a heavyweight fight, but I emerged victorious in the battle of projectile vomit on the aircraft. Walking down the jetway in New Orleans, I felt a surge of relief that I had never felt before. I cannot describe the euphoria I felt at that moment.

It was pure joy.

It did not last.

I went to dinner with my wife and young daughter when I got home. As soon as I finished dinner, the "asshole" was back – the surge of anxiety with the powerful urgency to puke. Of course, I was sitting in the rear corner of the restaurant, packed with Sunday night family dinners, and the bathroom was on the other side of the restaurant. Fuck me.

My eyes scanned the room with the intensity of a soldier behind enemy lines. My heart was pounding, my stomach was grumbling, and that damn sweet-tasting saliva was back.

Could I make it to the bathroom to puke?

Where is the front door?

Would it be wrong to push the emergency exit door and run out?

Do I tell my wife what is happening? No way. There was no chance she would understand.

Maybe I have a stomach virus, I thought.

"Shoot, this is what it felt like the other night at dinner at the conference when I thought I ate a bad appetizer," as I reflected on the painful events of the last few days. That night, I ran outside, then went to the bathroom and splashed cold water on my face. That helped.

If I try to go to the bathroom in this restaurant, how many people will I puke on before I get there?

I remember thinking I could vomit down my shirt as a better alternative than puking on someone's dinner. How ridiculous is that thought?

There is a plant over there. That may work.

The freaking sweet saliva is getting stronger!

I got up and walked very briskly to the front of the restaurant. I do not know why I chose that route, but before I knew it, I was standing outside. I do not remember the steps, the faces, or who I ran over to get free. I had to make it, and no one was safe unless they wanted to wear my vomit.

Knowledge is not Always Power

In my first year of graduate school, I had a professor teach about anxiety from a personal experience.

"We are going to be talking about anxiety. If you have never had a panic attack, do not judge those who have had one. Until you have one, you cannot understand the fear, pain, and misery of a panic attack. Just remember that."

Preach on.

That was my third panic attack in 48 hours. I had one in that restaurant when I thought I had eaten a spoiled appetizer. The second was on an airplane, and the third was in a restaurant with my family. Bad things come in threes, or so I have been told.

If you are reading this book, you probably know the pain of anxiety very intimately. If you don't have a history of anxiety, let me describe my anxiety to you, symptom by symptom.

My head pounded like I was sitting next to speakers from a powerful surround sound system set to max volume. The pressure and noise rose from the base of my skull.

My stomach was very volatile and nauseous. If you have ever had food poisoning, you know the inevitable feeling when there is no choice but to find a spot to find relief. I felt bloated, sick, and painful.

Unlike the balmy, sticky sweat from sitting in a sauna, my skin was soaking wet. Instead, it was a cold sweat, just on the surface of my skin. But my clothes were drenched.

My heart felt like I had been injected with adrenaline, pounding so hard that I worried that people could see my shirt moving or veins in my neck bulging.

That sweet taste of your saliva? Oh yes. I have no idea what that is, but it is powerful.

My mind was racing each time the anxiety spiked. Thoughts flooded my consciousness with plans to escape my environment, worries about what was happening, and intense fear of embarrassment or losing control. It is incredible how those thoughts can coexist at the same time.

I knew how to treat anxiety and panic attacks. At that point in my life, I had been treating patients with anxiety for several years, but it is different when it is not your personal terror. Sure, I wanted them to do well and feel better, but I was not "dying" inside with every breath or fearful moment of my life.

I had to learn to self-manage my *own* anxiety and find the right tools to endure the pain I was in, but at that moment, those options did not seem feasible.

My panic attacks kept going for a few days. The only way I knew to stop them was not to eat. I decided to eat at home, and if I had to go to a restaurant, I would drink water and eat very little. I was in survival mode. My goal was survival.

I never threw up with my panic attacks.

Not one time.

The decisions I started to make during one of the most challenging times of my life set the stage for everything that I do now. I had to learn a process to understand what I was experiencing and appreciate that the feelings, fears, and misery were just moments in time, not predictors of my future.

I have repeatedly heard that "what doesn't kill you makes you stronger," and I would have to agree now. Being crushed by anxiety makes you feel like you are dying, but I found that I could understand anxiety better, learn to appreciate its relationship with my body, and start to implement a plan to push through the pain. While the plan seems minor from the outside, any progress is positive when you are drowning in fear, fighting the crushing pain from anxiety, and questioning the comfort of your future.

Anxiety is not about getting over it but pushing through it.

The Beast

Our world is under attack by anxiety. It is an equal opportunity offender, and when it gets its grip on you, it will not let go. Anxiety is not dangerous or destructive in isolation, but it can wear you down when it has time to establish its roots in you.

You must understand that anxiety often attacks in two ways – like a tornado destroying everything in its path and like water eroding the foundations of a house.

The tornado represents panic attacks. Panic attacks typically come out of nowhere without warning and create tremendous damage. As fast as they come on, they suddenly move on. Generalized anxiety or worry is like water damage that starts slowly but eventually undermines your foundations, weakening you from the ground up.

Anxiety does not care who you are. It is an equal opportunity offender.

The truth is anxiety does have some benefits in your life. It can help you focus, prepare, and face challenges. The problem is how uncomfortable it makes you and how that builds with every struggle, frustration, and fear.

In sports, anxiety can help you get ready for big games. You have found yourself worrying about a big competition, only to work more efficiently, practice with greater intention the closer you get to the competition, and even focus on the right things. Those butterflies in your stomach need to start flying together!

I know many athletes who vomit before big games. One of my best friends ate Pepto Bismol like candy and had a very productive career in Major League Baseball. Every competitive athlete knows the feeling when their mind floods with doubts, insecurities, and fears.

Understand that anxiety in its purest form is not a problem. Anxiety becomes a problem when it changes your perspectives, gets physically uncomfortable, and negatively impacts your plan forward.

This book will give you the weapons to tame the beast of anxiety. In this book, you will have the tools to focus on the perspective around anxiety, managing how it makes you feel, and finding a positive path forward through every challenge you have. Anxiety does not have to be detrimental or destructive.

As an athlete, you can become a Hall of Fame competitor even if you have anxiety.

You can become the greatest athlete in your sport if you suffer from depression.

You can win a championship and suffer from panic attacks.

In life, you can have anxiety but continue functioning at a high level and living happily. You may not always feel your best, but you can perform at your best.

It is time to dispel the notion that mental health problems can either hold you back or cause problems. A challenge to your emotions or struggles to keep your confidence up does not mean you cannot succeed at your goals. Intense worry or troubles with depression do not predict a dire future.

Simply put, your mental health and overall wellness are not like light switches but beautiful complexities along a continuum of experiences, all housed in the expression of your mind. Those experiences are not "all or nothing" but rather levels of feelings, doubts, beliefs, and arousal.

Your mental health is like a gauge - times when it is overworked and overloaded and others when it is comfortable.

The hardest thing about working in the mental health space, particularly among athletes, is that you cannot fully appreciate how others are struggling. If you have a bad back, I could probably see the dysfunction on an X-ray or MRI, particularly if trained to see the problems.

If you have crippling anxiety, you can compete at a high level every day, and I would never know, even though you are suffering in silence.

One of my advisors, Dr. Justin Nash, gave me a piece of wisdom I carry daily. We were walking the fairways watching the PGA Tour and my players, and he said, "Remember, for you and your players, we cannot see another person's thought bubble above their heads."

Simple and profound.

I suffer from anxiety. I faced panic attacks in my fourth year of graduate school. I have battled them on occasion over the years when my stomach gets a bit queasy in a large gathering, a place I cannot escape, or when I am sitting on an expert panel.

I faced anxiety head on and learned more about myself than I imagined.

I made a choice that the pain, anger, and embarrassment would not own me anymore. I chose to face the beast and took control.

1

SETTING THE STAGE

I received a call from a coach late one Sunday night. As a national championship-winning coach, he built his program on toughness, structure, and preparation.

His competitors called him an "old-school" coach, a backhanded compliment implying he employed a coach-first, player-second style. Rival coaches and fanbases often use the "old-school" moniker as a criticism or deterrent to play for a coach who has high demands, trains hard, and gives direct feedback. There are coaches who try to be "old school" and are abusive, drive players into the ground, and do not establish positive relationships with players. Great coaches are often "old school," so I don't want to perceive this coach as abusive or ineffective. He was one of the most player-centered coaches I had worked with, and his call reflected his level of concern for his player.

"Hey Doc, I have a player who I cannot figure out. He has the tools but struggles in games and practice and seems disconnected from the team. I need help."

Messages like that from a coach are powerful.

When the player and I met, he was in an emotionally tough spot. He sat across from me in my office and looked like he was showing up for inquisition by the firing squad. With every word, he labored to find the next descriptor to offer some insight while keeping me far enough away from the problem to remain comfortable. I felt for him, even though, as a clinician, I needed to stay impartial and get to the bottom of the problem.

As a highly recruited player, he had played across the country in invitationals and was a sure-fire professional in his sport. Before arriving on campus, recruiting gurus had covered every match, game, and showcase, trying to connect the dots to their impact on the university.

Over the hour, I had established enough rapport that he let down his guard and let me into his suffering. For the past four years, he had been battling an internal war with anxiety, the obsessive, critical self-appraisals he was letting down his coaches, family, and fans daily.

This player was a pleaser and wanted his coaches to respect him, believe in him, and trust him. Yet, he didn't respect, believe in, or trust himself to do the job.

Throughout high school, this level of anxiety was manageable because he achieved significant success and acclaim on talent alone. The lower levels of anxiety would give way to perfectionism, and his coaches praised him for his work ethic and even used him as an example for younger players.

If he doubted his preparation, he trained more.

If he doubted his fitness, he would work out after practice. Coaches would post videos on social media, and the comments would complement his work ethic and his "superstar" desire. When he felt anxious, he just trained more. When he caught the attention of college coaches, they loved his level of "desire" because they wanted positive influences on their teams. During his recruiting process, one rival coach told me they recruited him solely to establish a championship-level work ethic in their program.

"You can't coach that. That is in his DNA."

No one knew the player's pain because of the worry and feelings of inadequacy across several aspects of his life.

This player did not know how to manage it. If he exercised harder, the pain went away for a period. Well, until his mind wandered and obsessed about someone else beating him.

He would go out with his friends and found that some beer and pot would help quiet his inner critic. That would last until he sobered up and felt immense guilt for doing stupid things.

When he arrived on campus, the inner critic took over.

How could he ever succeed here with so many great players?

What if he failed? What would his hometown say?

He had told everyone he dreamt of playing professionally, but that was untrue. He thought he hated the game, but instead, he hated the way the game made him feel.

His inner critic never let up. If he were lying down at night, the thoughts would intensify.

You are not doing what it takes to succeed.

Did you forget to send Coach your notes?

Did you forget an assignment for class?

Did you screw up at practice?

Did you like the wrong type of post on social media?

Even though none of his worries were true, as he was going to bed, they seemed 100% true. He would lie in bed for hours trying to calm his thoughts, slow his heart rate, or stop hyperventilating. Eventually, he would fall asleep, waking up at 530 in the morning for workouts. He was constantly tired and would fall asleep in meetings or tutoring sessions.

By the time he had gotten to me, he was a zombie. The referral came in his redshirt junior season, his fourth year on campus. He had been treading water for three years, doing everything he could to keep his head above water.

He didn't care that he was struggling because he could limit his mental engagement and effort in the game. His grades suffered, too. He didn't care that he did not have a girlfriend because who would want to date a guy with all his problems, or so he thought?

He was in survival mode and on the brink of breaking down.

Put yourself in his shoes for a minute. Throughout his high school career, he had been fighting anxiety but found that working harder made the worries disappear. The harder he worked, the more positive attention he got, and the better he played. The better he played, the more anxiety he got. So, all he knew to do was work harder.

Eventually, he couldn't keep up the pace and started to drown.

How would you handle that? Tell him to stop working so hard? Tell him to start anti-anxiety medication? While medication can help with some players, he was against taking medicine, so I need to explore better alternatives.

Not only was he stressed out, but he was also embarrassed, hiding his anxiety for as long as he could remember. He could put on a strong face, covering his worries by becoming the tough-talking, macho athlete persona.

My assessment made it clear he was suffering from anxiety, specifically generalized anxiety disorder and social anxiety disorder. The combination of generalized and social anxiety is not uncommon, but it is excruciating for someone who competes in front of large crowds. Social anxiety centers around the fear of negative appraisals from others. As an athlete, you cannot ever escape.

He told me he felt alone, isolated from the joy that others were feeling. He did not have the insight that others may be suffering, too.

I will highlight some treatment strategies we used later in this book. We worked together, including involving Coach at his request, to build a protective environment where he could challenge the inner critic and grow externally.

We went to work and saw a great response. He finished his collegiate career and plays professionally now. He told me he still battles the inner critic but found coping strategies that allow him to get relief. Most importantly, he knows he is not alone, confiding in his spouse and coaches that he fights this battle daily. The funny thing is his coach fights the same challenges with anxiety, so they have formed a strong bond, sharing strategies, readings, and even music that can soothe the stress.

It is Just Worry, Right?

Over the past decade, an essential focus has been on mental health and wellness in athletics. It has been very needed; I wish it had happened 50 years ago. But I am glad the focus is there now.

Depression has been in the spotlight and garnered the most attention. Anxiety has stayed in the background, but it has caused plenty of challenges.

People who suffer from anxiety are imprisoned in their minds, burdened by the "what if's" and the "should's" of life. The only perceived relief is the absence of anxiety, which is damn near impossible in any environment.

The Problem is Significant

When I started working in athletics, my goal was to raise awareness for mental health by helping athletes perform better on the field. I thought that if I helped athletes play better, I could open their eyes to the benefit of paying attention to their mental health.

For many years, coaching the mental side of the game was reserved for those in slumps, who had conflicts with the coaching staff, or who were deemed uncoachable. Getting referred to the sports psychologist was like being sent to the principal's office or shipped out for last-resort solutions.

The mental side of the game, including performance psychology and mental health treatment, is 30 years behind strength and conditioning. When I was competing in the 1990s, there was an emerging trend in strength training for individualized programming for each athlete. Before that, it was not uncommon for every athlete on a team to do the same workout, and it did not matter if you were a pitcher or an outfielder. Strength was strength, but then, coaches started to evaluate the individual needs of each athlete and tailor workouts to those needs. At that moment, strength and conditioning became constructive.

Athletes have long-standing relationships with their private strength coaches and performance trainers in today's game. Collegiate football players, like professional athletes, now arrive on campus with private training groups at home. That is not wrong, just that it shows the field's growth.

Mental coaching is still stuck in the corrective phase. Like in the 1990s, in strength and conditioning training, I would get some tailored exercises to strengthen my weaknesses if I had a bad back. People now find mental training when something is wrong, looking for a correction.

Mental training must become constructive, including mental health treatment and a focus on wellness. If an athlete has a positive experience with me and finds ways to improve their performance, I hope I have given them a positive experience should they ever need treatment.

It is time to shift our mindset toward Construction.

Black Socks and Sandals

"Who is the dude standing behind the batting cages?" My teammate asked.

"I have no idea. Is that guy a booster? He looks like one of the reporters. He has black socks up to his calves with brown sandals, so I doubt he is a coach or former player," I answered.
At our team meeting in the outfield before practice, Coach Skip Bertman, arguably the greatest college baseball coach of all time and winner of five national titles in 10 years, introduced the sock and sandal guy as a mental coach who wanted to watch us practice. He was in town and wanted to learn how a

championship team trained, and Coach offered him to any of us who wanted to talk to him for the day.

No one took him up on it. Coach Bertman sent one young player who struggled with adjusting to the speed of the college game to spend some time with him. Thankfully, Coach didn't send me over to the mental coach.

After practice, the poor player returned to the locker room and was speechless. He shared that the mental coach made him put things on his hat to find the pitched ball sooner and focus better between pitches. Before he knew it, he had two or three teaching tools on his hat and had to think about four or five different things with each pitch. He said that he got so frustrated and found that his eyes were crossing looking at the stupid thing on the bill of his cap.

Finally, he looked at the mental coach and asked, "Is this supposed to help?" The mental coach answered, "I believe so." At that point, the player asked, "Have you ever tried to hit a baseball?"

"No. But I watch a lot of baseball, and I think I can help you."

The player walked off.

Now, you don't have to play the sport you coach, but it helps to understand from the player's point of view.

I have always remembered that day because I never want to be seen as a guy wearing black socks with sandals, out of touch with the players I am trying to lead and making them more frustrated rather than helping. No doubt the mental coach believed he could help, and I give him that credit, but times have changed. When I started speaking to college teams over ten years ago, I could guarantee lively discussions if I presented on performance improvement. Conversely, if I gave a presentation on mental health – anxiety, depression, or substance abuse – I could speak for an hour, and maybe one player would approach me at the end of the presentation. I would get a few messages afterward along the lines of "Doc, that was great, but I didn't want to come up at the end because I didn't want anyone to know, but I have been suffering from anxiety for a few years. Thank you!"

Today, when I give a talk on a college campus, I have a coordinator attend the presentation who can schedule attendees for follow-up appointments and provide appropriate resources. I allocate extra time to answer questions. Instead of one random text, I average 20-30 players coming up to talk afterward, and they will wait in the presence of others. Something has changed.

There is a change happening, and it is needed. Mental health treatment and mental performance training are moving to the front of competitors' collective awareness. They no longer thrive in the darkness, hidden from public view due to shame and embarrassment. This change is not only necessary but may be life-saving.

Depression is no longer just feeling down, anxiety is not feeling nervous, and stress is not being overwhelmed.

This book is not a clinical textbook studying anxiety or a self-help book full of "the ten best strategies to defeat your ills." No, that is not what this is about, and I am not sure we need another one of those types of books.

I have wanted to write a book on anxiety and my struggles for some time. As a clinical and sport psychologist, I see anxiety in so many of my clients. Many are undiagnosed, having suffered alone, thinking their feelings were normal. Some take medication, which helps them find support early on in their suffering and seek me out to find solutions to help them stop taking medication.

I believe in the combination of medication and therapy if both are right for you. I have had periods where I have taken prescribed medication to help lower the volume of energy in my head and other times when I can function through my self-management skills. I believe both are important, depending on each patient.

I will share how I manage my anxiety, but this is also not a book about my "success over anxiety."

Nope.

This book is about understanding a strategy I used that may help you. I will share what has helped me so you can find your way to manage your anxiety in your life and your performance world. It is that simple. The strategy I learned was a sampling from a few different ideas, some stoicism, a little acceptance, and a lot of rationalizing my feelings, mixed in with training as a clinical psychologist with some of the most brilliant, innovative psychologists in the field of anxiety.

You are a living, breathing organism facing the challenges of today, influenced by your experiences and biases. Struggle doesn't mean you are failing, unable to compete or succeed in life—quite the contrary.

You must learn to shift your perspective away from surviving the pains of anxiety and towards the power of fighting through them.

I hope this book shapes your perspective and confidence to face the "what ifs" running you in circles and into the ground.

2

THE UNITED STATES OF ANXIETY, DEPRESSION, AND STRESS

Our world's poor perception of mental health was best captured by a grocery store check-out line in 2007. As I waited to check out my groceries, I saw two magazine covers that reflected our country's perceptions of mental illness and psychological suffering compared to other medical conditions.

On the front cover of *People Magazine* was the bald, freshly shaven head of pop princess Britney Spears. Her fall from grace was highlighted and celebrated in a circus-style gawking where the publisher presented her as a freak, sideshow, and tragic disaster. *People Magazine* appeared to have one goal in mind, and it wasn't seeing more people struggling with mental health issues seeking treatment. They wanted to sell magazines on the back of a celebrity struggling with a silent disease.

On the front cover of another magazine, which I cannot remember the name of for the life of me, was an actor from a nighttime blockbuster television show. The cover featured the actor smiling, proudly celebrating their survival and defeat of skin cancer. Yes, skin cancer treatment is a noble and vital cause, but the contrast between the treatment of the two conditions spoke volumes.

For decades, leaders, policymakers, commentators, and nearly everyone has ignored the actual suffering of mental health. Politicians never seem to find the necessary funding for mental health treatment, and health systems park their mental health departments in remote sections of their facilities only to remove treatment from their policies.

Policy leads to perspective.

Those who suffer have had to suffer in isolation, burying the pain of anxiety, depression, bipolar disorder, addiction, and other mental health conditions for fear of unnecessary judgment, ridicule, and rejection from our society. If you suffer from mental health issues, you do not have to stay in the shadows because society does not know how to interact with you – that is on them, not you!

Something has changed, however, within the past decade. I don't know where the wave of support changed, but I am not arguing.

Athletes have suffered in silence for years, often self-medicating with alcohol and drugs, since that appeared more acceptable than giving a press conference and disclosing a battle with depression. I remember talking to a friend in Major League Baseball who told me that they would put players on the disabled list for strained backs instead of listing depression. He also said they would not trade for or sign players with depression or significant anxiety because "the higher-ups do not believe they were strong enough to handle the pressure."

Amazing.

Royce White, the number 16 pick by the Houston Rockets in the National Basketball Association (NBA) draft, became the subject of intense media attention when it was disclosed that he had generalized anxiety disorder and suffered from a significant fear of flying. His fear of flying was so intense that he only wanted to be drafted by franchises that could accommodate his anxieties.

As a result, many franchises passed on White to not have to make those accommodations. Thankfully, White had a coach who went to battle for him, former NBA All-Star Kevin McHale, even though others strongly opposed the draft pick.

The media was not friendly, presenting an unsupportive and condescending picture of a complicated issue. White requested bus travel whenever possible, but the negotiations turned sour, with the Rockets delaying his signing and ultimately tainting the franchise on White. He never played significant time in the NBA, only having a brief stint with the Sacramento Kings.

Mardy Fish was a professional tennis player who rose to prominence in the worldwide tennis circuits, experiencing moderate success at the four tennis Majors early in his career. It wasn't tennis that brought attention to Fish, but rather an article on September 2, 2015, in *The Players' Tribune,* the online media platform for athletes to share their first-hand stories.

Fish shared his journey with anxiety and depression and how both have negatively impacted his career. It was the first of its kind, and for readers, a window in the suffering of a world-class athlete often shielded from the public's view.

The Players' Tribune may be the most crucial resource for destroying mental health stigma. They routinely feature powerful stories of recovery, suffering, and resilience from players, Hall-of-Famers, coaches, trainers, etc. The first-hand accounts have shown that you can succeed at the highest levels despite mental health challenges.

Imagine if Royce White was drafted just ten years later. Just think of how many athletes we have "lost" to drug and alcohol abuse, burnout, or "uncoachable" attitudes when mental health issues were raging inside them. All without the necessary services to help them overcome their internal struggles while giving all they had to produce for their teams and families.

Imagine if improved performance opened a window into the psyche of an athlete. What if an athlete met with a psychologist or mental skills coach to improve their on-field performance, which opened the possibility of sharing their traumas, fears, and insecurities? One window could open to an entire environment.

When I played baseball in the 1990s at LSU, finding a consulting psychologist or mental health provider affiliated with the athletic department was difficult. Thankfully, my mom was very engaged and close with a few psychologists in the area, and I would occasionally visit them. A mental performance coach in the community helped me unlock my abilities while I was playing, which turned me on to becoming a clinical psychologist.

It was the consensus back then that athletes would be better mentally because they were pursuing something they loved to do, playing a sport, and achieving their goals. If there were struggles, it was easier to conclude it was due to character flaws rather than mental health issues. They were resistant to coaching or needed to find a better environment if they could not be reached at their current school.

Data does not support these erroneous beliefs. Research from the American College Health Association (ACHA) has demonstrated that athletes experience rates of mental illness similar to their college counterparts. Through their National College Health Assessment survey methodology, the ACHA examines all aspects of healthcare among college students, regardless of whether they are college athletes or traditional students. Their data suggest that athletes are experiencing similar levels of stress, impairment, and significant concerns regarding suicidality as traditional students.

The NCAA, the governing body of intercollegiate athletics in the United States, has shifted significant resources in the past decade toward mental health. The NCAA's medical director, Dr. Brian Hainline, has spearheaded initiatives and worked to provide valuable consensus statements on providing mental healthcare on college campuses. Now, it is common to have multiple practitioners embedded within the athletic department instead of farming out said care to the student health center across campus. It is impossible to schedule student athletes for appointments due to their schedules, so embedding professionals has improved access and reduced the stigma of seeking help.

Over the past ten years, I have been fortunate to work directly with one of the pioneers, Dr. Ginger Gilmore, an athletic trainer who obtained a Doctorate in Behavioral Health to improve care for student-athletes at the University of Alabama. With her boss, Jeff Allen, Dr. Gilmore has been a valuable resource in facilitating care, triaging mental health emergencies, and communicating to coaches what players are experiencing. Coaches have been quick to rely on Dr. Gilmore and Jeff Allen to help players better, and there have been numerous anecdotal stories to validate the quality of care.

But this is not an NCAA issue. Our country and the entire world have been fighting an increased mental health burden over the past few years. In 2020 and 2021, the American Psychological Association (APA) surveyed American public members to assess stress levels in their lives. Because of factors such as the novel coronavirus (COVID-19) pandemic, social justice tensions and initiatives, and a contentious national political environment, 2020 and 2021 were the highest stress levels since the APA began the survey. These years have been greater than during World Wars or other international concerns.

If stress in America is growing, where does it go?

Increased alcohol consumption? Sure.

Drug abuse? Yes.

Violence? Absolutely.

Suffering? Without question.

Stress must go somewhere. It is like the support of a bridge. The bridge will function quite well if there is no weight on it. If the bridge becomes burdened by heavy trucks, the bridge must absorb and dispel the pressure somewhere. Architects and engineers have optimized construction design and support to distribute heavier weights on bridges effectively, but eventually, every bridge has a maximum capacity.

The human system is no different.

The resulting impact of carrying too much weight in life, too much stress even if it is positive, is on the body-mind complex of every human, also referred to as the psychophysiological system. Over time, greater exposure to stress will lead to breakdowns of your nervous, immune, and cardiovascular systems. Not to mention the burden incurred by your psychological system. Eventually, you will see more chronic physical illnesses, anxiety, depression, and related psychological/psychiatric illnesses.

We are in a new pandemic in this country – the mental health pandemic. As athletes, you are not immune to it, and I would argue, as you will read in this book, that you must learn to see your anxiety, depression, and stress differently. It is no longer about the warning signs of having anxiety (depression or any other condition), but now it is how to function with it at your best, and in doing so, you will kick anxiety's ass time and time again.

But Why Do I Worry? Me, Why Me?

There is a difference between full-on attacks from anxiety and the destruction caused by the relentless erosion from worry. If anxiety is the attack at the front gates of your compound, worry is like being infiltrated by spies working to destroy you from the inside out.

Worry is your mind's way of feeling productive when it cannot resolve the issue.

That is just the facts.

When your body and mind are under attack from increased arousal, your mind must respond. Your mind must find a solution to the problems or escape discomfort. Staying in the status quo is not good enough.

Worry is the mental gymnastics you go through to feel like you are making progress or working through a problem, but the problem has no immediate solution. If you could solve the problem, you would move on. The fact that you cannot is why you continue to worry. When you worry, you feel that you are doing something: doing something makes you feel better, but you are not doing anything productive spinning your mental wheels worrying.

You know that friend who tells you how much they work out, how many hours they train, or how much they must do every day, but you do not really care how much they do? It always seems they must tell you they did so much more than you, right?

That is like worry.

If your mind cannot immediately resolve the anxiety, it triggers more mental energy toward trying to solve the problems, but the problems will never go away. The fact that you are worrying is because you cannot resolve it where you are!

How much worry do you have when you are playing? In the biggest moments?

How much worry do you have when you are lying down at night and trying to go to sleep?

Think about that – worry attacks when you cannot solve the problem.

When you are in an environment where you can do something about it, the worry disappears, and you face the drama of the moment.

I love this quote about worry from the Dutch writer Corrie Ten Bloom:

Worrying is carrying tomorrow's load with today's strength – carrying two days at once.

It is moving into tomorrow ahead of time. Worrying doesn't empty tomorrow of its sorrow, it empties today of its strength.

Worrying does not solve problems. Imagine using the energy you create when you feel powerless to fix your anxieties and devote that to planning to attack the next moment you are in. Why expend your energies living in the future when the moment you are in demands everything you can possibly summon together?

3

SO, ANXIETY DEVELOPS?

"What the hell happened to me, doc?

I used to be so confident and felt so strong in the games. I knew I would find a way to win, and now I am crushed by fear."

Tommy was a college pitcher with professional aspirations. Frankly put, he was a stud. Agents and professional scouts drooled over him every time he pitched.

"Surefire, first-rounder with Major League talent. He will pitch for many years if he stays healthy," one agent told me.

Another was attracted to his physical presence on the mound, likening him to Max Scherzer, the perennial All-Star and genuine pitching bad ass.

Once Tommy got to college, he lost his mental edge. School was tough, the competition amongst the pitching staff was deep, and he needed help finding self-confidence. Moving away from home was tough, too. His parents used to go to every game he pitched, and there was peace of mind seeing their calming presence.

Now, his coaches told him things he had never had to deal with.

They were tweaking his mechanics and scrutinizing his performances.

"Where is that guy we recruited?" they asked.

The harder he tried, the worse he performed.

Anxiety began to build. His mind flooded with thoughts and fears of "losing me" and not becoming the player everyone thought he should be. The pitching mound sparked so much anxiety that his body became tight, his heart pounded through his jersey, and he lost all his rhythm.

He started to lose sleep, waking up throughout the night worried about letting down his friends, losing the trust of his coaches, and disappointing his agent/advisors. Anxiety was destroying him.

The "can't miss prospect" was a disaster, and there was no hope. Coaches were talking about transferring as a mechanism to find his confidence again, and his parents recommended taking a year away from the game.

He was living in a world of nightmares and lost his confidence.

I hate it when that happens. I see it often, particularly when athletes move up levels, go to college, or take on new responsibilities like becoming a starter. The changes open the window for anxiety to build, and that anxiety takes every opportunity to create havoc.

I recognize it because I know it personally.

The sensations are unmistakable, driven from deep in my core and permeating every extremity of my large-framed body. I usually first feel it in my stomach, a queasiness different from any uncertainty I feel before something challenging. It is more than that, to be honest.

Anxiety is a part of my life. I would love to tell you that anxiety is a part of my past, but that would be a lie. I live every day with elements of anxiety.

Yet, I am the clinical and sport psychologist the top performers in the world hire when they want help with their struggles.

That irony is the beautiful drama of anxiety. It is an equal opportunity offender and does not relent with success. Anxiety should go away when threats, challenges, and struggles revolve, but seem to increase with each success.

Anxiety builds on past traumas and intensifies with increased responsibilities as you prepare to face the next challenge – known or unknown. For me, the unknown challenges are the most difficult to manage.

I do not always know why my anxiety intensifies. It often starts with a seemingly innocuous stressor, something that is usually not an issue until it is in that moment. From that moment forward, my mind races with thoughts, worsening with every fear and doubt, until I feel significant heaviness in my chest and shoulders. As those feelings intensify, my mind catastrophizes, resulting in a more negative outlook and frustration that changes my mood into a negative burden of stress.

The problem is that simple breathing techniques and other dime-store techniques do not work. My anxious mind is too powerful for simple treatments.

Why do I feel this way?

Why do I make it hard on my wife and kids?

How can I keep up a positive appearance for my clients?

The questions are never about what to do, however. Those questions seem minor compared to the pain of anxiety, and the need to manage the immediate moment takes precedence.

As my anxiety builds, it ramps up through the physical pains and shifts towards a fatalistic mindset. It is hard to see the positive when the hurt of anxiety is so hard.

And then, in a few days or weeks, the pain's intensity diminishes. Something happens that shifts my mindset, an awareness of the reality that suggests that things are better than the depth of my fears. With each experience, I know how to learn about anxiety and how it builds in me. That is the lesson that anxiety brings to me now.

I find my anxiety moves in stages through my body. The sensations may start in my body, but typically, my mind has been on full alert for some time. I obsess about inconsequential factors, worrying that someone is upset with me, or that I have not performed adequately for a client. I want to think it is silly, but in my mind, it is real.

The early worries led to more sensations in my body, specifically my gut. I cannot explain the feeling in my stomach more than just topsy-turvy. Not *really* nausea, but not at peace. There is a tumbling, gurgling, and sometimes, a crampy sensation that tells me something is not right but not *really* wrong. I struggle to describe the indescribable.

How do you know something is wrong if your senses tell you things may be wrong but not bad, just not right?

That is *the* creation of anxiety.

It is like when a hurricane forms in the Gulf of Mexico. What starts as a poorly formed aggregate of tropical storms morphs into a powerful, organized, and sometimes devastating storm.

My little worries, independent of one another, start to find connections, and before I know it, a storm is brewing in my head. My anxiety builds in the following stages:

1. Anticipation

The earliest phase of the anxiety experience happens deep below the surface. You can sense something is happening, but putting your finger on it can be difficult.

It is like a 6-year-old in the lead-up to Christmas morning. The closer they get, the more excited they become. They find an entirely different energy level and cannot listen, pay attention, or sit still. That is normal and expected. When it comes to anxiety, those same feelings seem to be seen negatively.

Anticipation is a weird experience. You bubble up inside, feeling the feels, but you cannot always understand what it is.

"What if" drives this phase. Your mind is constantly scanning, looking for threats.

Uncertainty is the greatest threat to your mind. You can never know what will happen in the future, and that is stressful for the mind, which primarily aims to protect you against those dangerous threats. Your mind triggers thoughts to identify threats and prepare you for those challenges.

Thoughts work like a radar, scanning your internal and external world for threats, assessing the depth of the dangers, and trying to prepare you for the challenges. The mind does not care if a thought makes you overreact or feel too worried about a benign risk. No, it just wants to scare you to pay attention.

With each thought that causes an emotional reaction or grabs your attention, your mind sends more thoughts related to the one that hit the target. But it digs in with greater intensity or description. The fact you had an emotional reaction, such as frustration or even trying to suppress that negative thought, tells the mind that it is hitting the danger zone.

With each negative thought that hits the target, the mind zeroes in more and more. Those on-target negative thoughts link together, and your mind amps up, anticipating the danger and preparing you for the threat.

Negative thought patterns tell stories, complete with the drama and risks taking centerstage.

Anticipation prepares you for something, but what that "is" is unknown. Your mind does not care that you overreacted; it just cares that you reacted.

2. Awareness

There is a difference between knowing something is happening and being aware of its existence and influence on you. During any day, your mind must take in millions of pieces of information, most entirely inconsequential for your existence. Many random bits of information would exist whether you were there or not, like a conversation happening at an adjacent table in a coffee shop. The patrons' discussion is happening no matter who sits next to them. Just because you are sitting there, the conversation is drawing your attention.

While Attention is the first step of Awareness, anxiety begins to grow during your mind's awareness of the building anxiety. Once something grabs your attention, your mind must understand the depth of the opportunity or threat, but a threat will always take precedence.

Awareness as a psychological skill will be one of the decisive steps to defeat the negative impact of anxiety. Still, your awareness contributes to the pain and discomfort as the discomfort builds. How can something so powerful, taught by so many in my field, also contribute to the negative impact of anxiety?

Simple.

Awareness must be heightened throughout life because the early identification of threat can be life-saving. Your mind cannot risk the consequences of missing a threat, exposing you to undue pain and suffering because it missed the early signs of trouble. Therefore, awareness must be primed for early identification at all costs.

Your anxiety builds because your mind is so effective at being aware of any threat – no matter the severity. The more anxiety you experience, the better you identify potential threats.

The problem is due to the efficiency of your awareness. Because you have gotten good at identifying threats and being aware of the feelings and sensations earlier, your general awareness becomes more tuned, identifying anything and everything, capturing your attention, and hijacking your awareness.

Awareness is not a multichannel process. The power of awareness is that your attention zeroes into the entire experience at the expense of other competing stimuli. Awareness is an "all-in" phenomenon.

You live in such a chaotic, hectic world that you never stop long enough to be aware of what you are feeling, thinking, and doing, as when your awareness becomes hijacked by threats, you lose your balance. Threats become the primary focus of your awareness, and your internal balance becomes lost. That is the truth.

Competing in sports only makes balanced awareness more difficult. Playing competitive sports requires so much mental energy and must compete against so many demands that the threats must be powerful to grab the full power of your awareness.

As you become more aware of the internal conflicts, the external threats, and the imbalance between them, your anxiety starts to fire up, elevating your arousal levels. Awareness simply raised the flag that something was wrong. It never said *what* was wrong, *why* it was wrong, or *how* things will play out. The better you get at identifying the imbalances and conflicts, the better you get at sparking the anxiety inside you.

3. Arousal

Now, let me review some of the basic physiology of the body's arousal system that shows up as anxiety. This section is not meant to be a comprehensive review of human physiology. Plenty of books, articles, and videos will describe that in detail. I want to take this section to examine the arousal stage from a first-hand account.

You use energy to drive your attention and fuel your activity in the face of challenges and opportunities, both real and imagined. That energy is adrenaline, a neurochemical that stokes the inner fire to respond to threats, sustain action, and consume every element of you when needed. You know that feeling when you are so excited to compete, pumped up by the fire inside you, and you cannot sit still? That is that inner fire I am talking about.

But anxiety feels just like excitement – particularly the physical feelings. The difference is how you perceive it mentally. The energy, or arousal, has so much power that the body and mind are constantly working in concert, trying to predict events in the future for you to be ready. When you can place the source of arousal as excitement or fear, your mind shifts into its default setting – anxiety.

There is a fine line between excitement and anxiety about arousal, and it centers on how you perceive the threat, challenge, or opportunity in the awareness phase. Your arousal will spike should you need the energy, but how it is utilized or diffused is beyond the scope of the arousal phase.

This stage is the fuel for your body and mind to do work.

Arousal is the fire driving the engine. Total immersion in the moment.

When I experience anxiety, I feel like my body is running in overdrive, and I cannot get a break. I find that I have significant muscle tension in my shoulders and chest, and my heart is beating out of my chest. Strangely, I do not find increases in measurements of my heart rate or blood pressure, so that fact makes it feel bizarre. I have more energy, but in turn, I feel heavier in everything I do.

The arousal that I feel seems to prepare me to face the challenge or threat, but I find it difficult to land on *exactly* what that threat is. My mind uses the energy to search and identify the stressors but never seems to stay focused on one need. Instead, the increased energy bounces me from point to point, threat to threat.

I told my wife during one period of anxiety that I feel the internal pressure building to face something very important, but that threat is always unknown. As the urgency intensifies, the conflict becomes challenging.

I can function with that conflict, but it is so difficult. My body and mind must adapt to the feels, but it is difficult to persist with the discomfort.

Athletes often share with me that they have attentional issues, like attention deficit disorder, during bouts of anxiety. Their attention and awareness become overrun, robbing their ability to sustain focus at practice or in games. If it has competing demands, that same arousal that can be used to get them ready to play will become lost on too many challenges, only to lose focus when it matters the most.

New bursts of arousal in response to novel threats demand the most attention. When the same threats continue to show up, the same feels continue to exert their feelings. The body must adapt to the threats. They lose their potency to grab your attention. If you didn't adapt to the similar feels, you would never advance.

4. Adaptation

I have noticed an interesting phenomenon when coaching athletes from today's generation - they are generally multitaskers. Players often listen to music while having multiple conversations at one time. I struggle to follow one of their conversations, much less two to three simultaneously.

"Doc, you just aren't good at getting used to things like we are," one of my players told me.

Fair enough. I am older than this player, and there is no doubt that the older I get, the harder it is for me to multitask. She was good at managing two or three things at a time. I thought that was so cool until I realized I do the same thing.

When I write, I listen to music, watch television, and often sit at a coffee shop. I need multiple levels of distraction to help me direct my attention to what matters. All those distractions drown out in the background.

That is what happens to arousal. Your attention shifts to something else, and your body adapts to the increased energy levels.

Does it go back to "normal"? No.

That is the issue with anxiety. You can function with it but rarely return to a relaxed state. You learn to function despite it.

Over time, the buildup of anxiety grows, only to continue to manage identified threats from multiple attacks. Your adaptation becomes more difficult.

The presence of arousal demands that my body and mind adapt to what it is feeling. I cannot simply stop because I feel amped up. I must adapt to what I am feeling.

Adaptation takes the feels and funnels those into function. If you cannot adapt to what you are feeling, then you will get paralyzed by fear and anxiety.

Adaptation is where many struggle. You cannot accept what you are feeling. If you were to see negative emotions and heighten arousal as a sign that you are not ready to compete, that it would cause problems, then of course you would see those feels as negative.

Let me explore Adaptation with you from the perspective of competitive stress.

The competitive arena does not have a standard level of feeling. Your feelings in the bottom of the ninth inning of a baseball game will feel different than in the fourth inning. The bottom of the ninth will also feel different in the World Series than in a midweek game in June.

Too many athletes feel that they should have the same feeling, and when they struggle with the new feels, they fail to adapt.

Imagine you are climbing a mountain. With the highest altitude, the top of the mountain will feel different than the bottom when you are chilling out at base camp. The top of Mount Everest will feel different than the top of any other mountain in the world. At over 29,000 feet elevation, the air is thinner, and your body struggles with such limited oxygen. But you may not need an external oxygen source at the top of Pikes Peak in Colorado, standing at just over 14,000 feet.

If you have been to the top of Mount Everest several times, you are more likely to be comfortable with the demands on your body and mind than the first time you attempt to summit the mountain.

Adaptation is not about ignoring or overcoming what you feel. It is about progressing despite what you feel. It is the power of the Pivot, being mentally flexible. This will be covered in more detail later in the book.

The biggest mistake with anxiety is that we try to prevent it and keep it at arm's length instead of realizing that it is just a "discomfortable" feeling. Yes, I said discomfortable because uncomfortable implies a lack of comfort, but when in the fire of anxiety, there is nothing lacking at all. It is only pure discomfort.

Anxiety will make you better, and it is not something to be afraid of.

Will Anxiety Overtake Me?

The challenge of anxiety is that the physical discomfort is only a portion of the struggle you experience mentally. To me, the physical symptoms are just a slight reflection of the turmoil inside your head.

Anxiety will not defeat you. You must understand why it is happening, how it builds, and what you can do to defeat it. Anxiety does not want you to succeed. Fear and doubt will tell you that you cannot handle the dangers and threats in the future.

You must start seeing yourself progressing through the bullshit without giving in to the pain or bleak future. You are not powerless and not broken.

If you buy into the fear that you are broken or incapable of enduring the pain of anxiety, you will only attract more trouble. You will see struggle as proof you cannot endure or overcome the challenges. Anxiety wants you to see areas of deficiencies as a mechanism to correct the flaws, as perverse as that seems.

If you do not think you will endure, you will prove yourself correct, time and time again. If you see success, you just might achieve it. Begin to see yourself standing up to the storm, and the clouds will pass over your head.

Imagine if you could hire a motivational coach or someone like me for every challenge in your life. That would be cool, wouldn't it?

I bet you would see someone there encouraging you, giving you the strength to push forward no matter what happens around you. Even if they told you that the next few months would be difficult, I bet you would rally every resource to face it because they would be standing there with you.

The motivational coach would overlook your weaknesses and past struggles, highlighting why you could endure the difficulty. You would work to prove them right!

Now, what would happen if they produced a fantastic highlight reel of every accomplishment you had ever achieved, showcasing your tenacity and endurance? After watching that video, you would be so pumped up that you could run through a brick wall.

Anxiety would not stand a chance against you!

If you begin to focus on what you want to achieve despite the challenges, you can serve as your own motivational coach. It isn't easy to see the positive capabilities in our own lives. The mind is built to highlight the dangers to protect us physically and emotionally. It is easier to motivate someone else than ourselves.

You must begin to see your value in the moment and your strength in standing up to anything. I have no idea what the future will hold, but I know you can endure any fear you have concocted in your mind. All I am asking you to do is increase the probability of success in your life. You can increase the odds despite having anxiety.

Tommy rebuilt his game and found strength in embracing his anxiety. While everyone had a plan, no one had relief from the anxiety he was suffering from. Doctors wanted him to take medication, and friends filled his inbox with meditation apps and quick fixes.

"Doc, I am bigger than my anxiety. I am more than what I feel. I will learn to become what I want, not live in fear of what I have become."

Those powerful statements embedded in a text shifted Tommy's mental perspective. The mere presence of anxiety did not predict his troubles.

Through our work, Tommy embraced the power of his anxiety and channeled that arousal to become a builder of his game, not a protector of his potential. Instead of being a victim of the changes in his life and the mental struggles, we worked on facing what was happening, not living the past or the lost future.

"What can I do right now despite how I am feeling?"

"What do I feel, and what can I focus on? Anxiety or intention – that is my choice."

Tommy had to change his mindset and accept that anxiety builds in competition and life. That is a fact. The presence of discomfort did not predict a bad future. He adapted to what he was experiencing and learned to become aggressive to his intentions.

Tommy is currently playing minor league baseball and thriving. The changes to his professional career were seamless, but only because he used the struggles of going to college as a lesson.

4

THE INCOMING TSUNAMI

"If you love your sport, you will never struggle. You must love it and be in love with the process."

I hate this sentiment. Statements like this crush competitors, not build them up.

Sara was in tears. After a difficult practice training session, her coach questioned her commitment to the game. Sara could not understand why her commitment and effort were now the focus of the criticism.

Sara was a talented athlete. For many years, the game was fun and relatively easy. Throughout high school, she played several sports and stayed active in school extracurriculars. She was popular within her friend group and was well-liked amongst other friend groups.

When she started college, she got overwhelmed quickly. Every day, she had a new meeting on her schedule, from compliance to academics, and then had to find time to train. Even though her sport was primarily a spring sport, her fall training was intense. That is common among college sports. Off-season training is often more intense than in-season training because it is the best time to drive performance improvements without competitive stress interfering with those changes.

For any new college athlete, the first semester on campus is like drinking from a fire hydrant. So many life changes are coming at one time that are often overwhelming. The individual demands alone can be fun, but when grouped together, I have watched players emotionally drown in those first semesters.

High school has a rhythm to it. By the time you are a senior, your class load lessens, and the extracurricular activities are busy but not exhausting. That changes in college.

Sara was emotionally exhausted.

As an admitted perfectionist, Sara thrived with order and predictability. Her freshman year had been a challenge. She was staying up late at night to study and waking up before the sun's first light to be in the water for her morning training. Three months in, she looked like a zombie.

After a challenging day in the water, her coach questioned her commitment to the sport.

"Do you love this? Because if you don't, maybe this isn't for you!" was the challenge that morning.

"The greats love their sport. It is simple as that."

Sara could not get over that question. Her mind became under attack by more perfectionism and stress. She was trying to do everything right and was being questioned about her commitment to her sport. Thoughts started to amplify, and doubts began to bury her.

Her doubts were powerful because no one was there to challenge them effectively. Every thought she had seemed to center on falling short and not reaching her potential, which was why she was recruited in the first place – she had the potential to be great. But did she have to *love it*?

She loved it in high school. Competition was fun then. Being one of the best athletes in her state helped her have more fun, and training was more fun. Fun was hanging with her friends and socializing. Now, she was training with a group of other zombies.

It was not like it is right now, she thought. How do you love misery?

> *Her mind was flooded with fears, too. Things like:*
>
> *If I fail here, what will my friends back home think?*
>
> *How can I get good grades when I can barely study? How will I take classes in my major when I can't even handle the pressure of first-year classes?*
>
> *What is tomorrow going to be like? Today was brutal, and I heard coach say tomorrow will be a table-setter. What is that?*
>
> *Does my coach think I hate the sport? Why would he say that? Am I letting coach down?*

The cascade of thoughts moved to a hypersonic flood of negativity, fears, and doubts. Some athletes do not get more anxious in those settings, as they can simply cope with and deal with the demands. Others, like Sara, are fertile ground for anxiety to grow out of control. The volume of her thoughts was significant, but she needed the right type of environment to cause the onset of uncomfortable struggles.

Sara had anxiety before arriving on campus, but the new demands and the unrelenting schedule only intensified her perfectionism. In working with today's athletes, I find this is the most common contributing factor to the rise in anxiety. I call it The Negative Triad.

The Negative Triad

Sara wanted to be a collegiate swimmer her entire life. She had seen friends and teammates leave her high school and club teams to swim in college and share the positive side of college swimming. As they talked about the fun side, Sara studied how they trained, the individualized elements of their sport, and measured herself against those standards. College swimming is just the start. Her family and coaches believed she could compete nationally and internationally. Training at the college level would only propel her forward, or so everyone thought.

That is the problem.

The Negative Triad is the formulation that I see in so many athletes and leads to very uncomfortable anxiety levels. It is the combination of unrealistic standards mixed with high levels of perfectionism and no breaks from the grind. Each one alone is fine, but when you get all three rolling, you have a model that cannot maintain progress for long. Eventually, you will overwhelm your coping mechanisms.

Astronomical Standards and Expectations

The standards and expectations are simply out of whack in today's sports.

If you are good at baseball, then you should emulate Mike Trout.

If you are good at golf, then Tiger Woods is your model.

What about tennis? Well, study Serena Williams, Roger Federer, Rafael Nadal, or Novak Djokovic.

If you want to study business and entrepreneurship, then study Sara Blakely, Gary Vaynerchuk, or Elon Musk.

Let's be honest, those are the perfect people to study. Do what they do, and you can succeed at that level, too. Right?

Wrong.

Those individuals, among many others whom I have not included, are some of the most significant outliers in the history of their endeavors. Sure, there are traits to study and behaviors to emulate, but do not measure yourself against their outcomes. Many factors contributed to their success, and you can never ignore timing, luck, and good fortune that increased the odds of their success. They are successful far beyond luck, but sometimes, good things open doors for certain people.

Those expectations are not just self-inflicted but accumulate from well-meaning coaches, parents, and outsiders. College students get consumed with landing the "perfect" job at a top company from the minute they start school, constantly jockeying for ranking positions to better their attractiveness to companies. High school students are adding classes to improve their grade point averages. It is no longer a 4.0 – you must push close to a 5.0 to be worth anything. Standardized tests quickly became the litmus test for getting accepted to the right colleges, despite consistent literature over the years that standardized tests like the ACT or SAT do not effectively predict college success.

You suffer from it, too. No one has the right to improve over time, not in this world. You have to perform great from the start, or you do not have what it takes. No wonder why the most common anxiety that I hear from so many of my athletes is "Am I *really* good enough?"

Society lost the perspective to celebrate improvements over time. Now, either you are good enough from the start or not. No wonder anxiety is running wild. Anxiety builds when standards cannot be met, but you must continue pushing to try unless you accept you simply aren't good enough.

Those unrealistic standards feed into perfectionism.

Perfectionism

Perfectionism is good until it is not.

There are elements behind a perfectionistic mindset that have value in high-performance settings, so I always reject the belief that perfectionism is a problem. Self-described perfectionists tend to be high performers, driving out doubts by devoting their energies to improving each aspect of their performance on things they can or believe they can control. That drive to control helps you work around issues by finding solutions that may not usually exist, pushing past resistance to solve a challenge.

In fact, if you were to interview a surgeon, pilot, nuclear power plant engineer, or musician, would you reject them because they described themselves as a perfectionist? Absolutely not, and you would probably rest easier if someone in charge was obsessive about the details.

The problem is that over time, the perfectionist exerts so much energy into the details that they can lose themselves trying to control every element of an outcome.

The risk is trying to control the uncontrollable. It is impossible not to make a mistake, never to struggle, or never have to deal with the drama of difficulty. There is a dramatic difference between being so driven by excellence that you exhaust all your energies versus being so anxious about making a mistake that you become paralyzed by difficulty. Both are in the realm of perfectionism but have a different motivation.

Most perfectionists start with the simple desire to be excellent. They want to get better at their sport, get good grades, and be the best at what they do. They improve their processes, eliminate the clutter, and avoid the mental traps that often cause problems for their colleagues. Early on, they feed off that attention and adoration, strengthening the skills that drive their performance.

Eventually, their level of performance moves them into new domains, against tougher competition, and in settings where they cannot control the factors around their outcomes. Perfectionists try harder as they lose control, searching for additional areas to gain traction, and rejecting times when they fall short of their goals. Those shortcomings become a rejection, creating a painful emotional vacuum from the original adoration that drove them at the outset.

That is when perfectionism becomes problematic.

"My coach wanted me to visit with you because I am a perfectionist. I cannot let go of a bad performance."

Take a step back for a second and look at that statement.

It is not about accepting a bad outcome, but in today's competitive culture, shortcomings are seen as immediate areas for correction, reflections of falling short of the ideal, and urgent remediation.

As a society, perfectionism has become the ideal. From the constant bombardment of social media posts reflecting near-perfect pictures to glorifying the elites in sport who never seem to miss, the short attention spans of our public do not reflect the patience to see growth. It does not matter that social media is never genuinely accurate or tells the whole story. The message becomes that you must be damn-near perfect in your physical appearance, grades, performance, and social settings to be considered an "influencer," whatever that means.

Therefore, pressure is so high currently. The massive standards feed right into the perfectionistic mindset, an adaptive shift honed to overcome the masses, the "average," and those left behind in a pursuit to become one of the "elite." That constant bombardment of perfect is exhausting.

No Downtime

When I was playing baseball in high school, I could have played baseball 12 months of the year, seven days a week. I loved being at the ballpark. Baseball never interfered with my academics because I did what I had to do to become an A-B student. Looking back, I probably underachieved in my academics, but everything worked out.

Societal demands, particularly within high-performance academics, sports, and extra-curricular environments, are overwhelming our youth. Adults are also overwhelmed, working 50+ hours per week, managing multiple schedules, and crashing on the weekend, bouncing between cities for "showcases."

Humans were not really built for this. If you look back at our ancestors, over the past 150 years, humans were optimized when a "hard day's work" was put in, and at night, you decompressed after dinner and turned in early. They may have worked six days per week, but they did not have a phone attached to their hand that constantly primed their minds to be on.

While the iPod is one of the most innovative products of our lifetime, it has led to a level of productivity crushing our mental health. The iPod led to the iPhone and all the brilliant productivity, connectivity, and efficiencies, but it also led to having a computer with you 24 hours per day.

As a result of being "on" all the time, attention spans are decreasing rapidly. Content is consumed on smaller screens than ever, and popular streamed shows are now "dumped" instead of staggering across the season. Live sporting events are watched with fans' heads buried in their phones.

During the 2022 PGA Championship at Southern Hills in Tulsa, Oklahoma, a viral photo grabbed the attention of Miller Brewing. Tiger Woods, the greatest golfer to ever play the game, was competing on his significantly damaged leg after his near-fatal car crash in February of 2021.

Every time Tiger competes, he draws the largest crowd on the course and drives television ratings. Rightfully so. Tiger is the best, and if you get the opportunity to watch, you do.

Yet, as Tiger was hitting a shot out of rough, just off the fairway, a photo was circulated with the gallery all fixed on filming Tiger on their phones, all except one man – Mark Radetic of Missouri. He just stood there, holding his Michelob Ultra beer, watching Tiger. Captured and distributed on social media, it went viral because it contrasted today's norm.

Not only did it hit on social media, but Michelob Ultra also made Radetic part of their advertising campaign just because he was watching live golf!

When you combine unattainable standards with perfectionism and never take time off, no one would love their sport. If they loved everything they did, I would be very concerned.

Something must bear the brunt of the overwhelming angst. Your coping systems are unprepared for such demands as they were not built for this. Not in the way they are being asked to work now.

Exhaustion leads to more perfectionism and a desire to control all factors. Exhaustion drives the Negative Triad.

When you are under constant stress, your mind interprets stress as a constant threat. You are living on high alert all the time. With each anxiety identified, you get better at identifying more threats. But you do not get better at identifying which ones will genuinely cause you problems.

Athletes play year-round, compete much more often than before, and have to manage multiple demands every day. There are pressures to get the highest ACT scores, get the best scholarships, and turn professional as soon as possible.

If you are taking a week off, someone else is training. While that is true, it is not healthy. You need time away from your sport. Your threat identification systems get most of your energy and attention when under constant stress. Threat only sees more threat.

Eventually, this cycle wears you down, leading to feeling helpless and hopeless.

The novelty of the situation is uncertain. To protect you from unknown threats, the mind must tell you that the future will be troubling instead of being difficult, hard, or challenging. Troubling and dangerous have no room for interpretation; you must be prepared. If you knew the future was difficult but safe, you would not have the same level of anxiety. But you never really know things will be safe, so you lose your ability to be flexible because you must evaluate every threat possible. There is no room for failing to identify the dangerous threats in the future.

The problem is that you start to draw connections. You connect feelings to future events.

"If I play poorly, I will play worse the next time. People would not like to watch me play or won't trust me if I am a bad player."

Those connections are the issue.

How fast do you go down that fear slide? Very fast. That is automatic.

When immersed in fear and anxiety, you don't think of solutions or strategies. You only think of survival, which ignores the tools you need to succeed.

You are not weak for having negative thoughts or fear. You are not out of balance spiritually or emotionally. You are a human facing uncertainty.

Those fears and doubts in the heat of the moment do not tell you that you will fail. They only tell you that things will be difficult.

The presence of anxiety does not mean you cannot handle it. The presence of anxiety means you are in a learning environment.

5

CALLING AN AUDIBLE ON ANXIETY

Ryan Holiday.

Stephen C. Hayes, Ph.D.

Susan David, Ph.D.

Mark Manson.

These authors opened my mind to see my anxiety differently. Through their unique perspectives, individualized vocabularies, and personal journeys, I gained additional insight into my anxiety and shaped my perspective going forward.

I have been very effective at keeping the pain of anxiety away from others. If you asked my wife, she would probably tell you that she knows I suffer from anxiety and worry way too much and that it is just who I am, but she would also tell you that she understands the depths of my struggle simply by living life with me. She knows when I am struggling and can feel the heaviness of my anxiety.

Each of the authors mentioned above explores different manners of human suffering. Those individualized perspectives resonated with me.

Ryan Holiday is the author of numerous books, notably *The Obstacle is the Way*, a modern philosophical analysis of stoicism, the ancient intellectual perspective of former Roman emperor Marcus Aurelius, Seneca, who was an advisor to the emperor, and Epictetus, who was a slave. I was fortunate enough to spend time with Holiday when he was a guest on my podcast, *The Secrets to Winning*, and we have stayed in touch over the years.

In our conversation, Holiday asked me, "Is there anything you cannot face?" Having read his books and listened to numerous podcasts on stoicism, it was not a new question, but rather, I was in a better position to listen. Stoicism emphasizes shifting your mindset from "what can happen" to "what can I do when it happens," or so that is my interpretation. In other words, I can be a great person instead of fearing all the negative things that could adversely impact me.

I often overlooked who I was, my intentions, and how I intended to treat people for fear of the future. The pain of tomorrow robbed me of my truth of my moments. Holiday's simple question and influential books shifted my lens on life.

Stephen C. Hayes, Ph. D., is a psychologist who trained at the same internship I did – the Clinical Psychology Training Consortium at Brown Medical School. While he trained a few years before me, he is widely considered a trailblazer in the field due to his work on Acceptance and Commitment Therapy (ACT). ACT is a slight shift from traditional Cognitive Behavioral Therapy (CBT), which emphasizes controlling irrational thoughts to change unhealthy thought patterns that lead to destructive behaviors or patterns.

ACT does not require the level of mental energy to change longstanding patterns; instead, ACT empowers individuals to be aware of the happenings in their inner and external world and find a healthier response despite those happenings.

Despite being trained in CBT, like me, Hayes found the power to pivot away from negative thoughts but not *change* them. Like having an annoying friend in your friend group, you must be prepared to be annoyed and have a simple plan not to let the irritation fester and grow.

Pivot.

Susan David, Ph. D., is also a psychologist and emphasizes in her writings and book *Emotional Agility* to respond to life's challenges with courage, despite what you feel. Emotions are just there and do not have to be the sole reason to act a certain way. "So what if you feel a certain way?" and find a different way to manage the discomfort.

Finally, Mark Manson is a blogger and author of the bestseller, *The Subtle Art of Not Giving a F&ck*. With an engaging title, Manson's book caught my attention with the promise of not caring what others think. Come to find out, the title is different from what the book prescribes. I found it to be a brilliant book to understand that there is nothing that I will face that I need to worry about in the future. In other words, who cares what could happen because I will face it.

So what?

There is no reason to fear the future if I can face whatever shows up.

Each of these authors highlighted a shift in my mindset that I want to share with you.

The pivot.

Agility.

Stoic.

Not caring.

Most importantly, I was ready to be mentally flexible.

So, What If I Get Fired?

I began to view anxiety differently about five years ago after I started to have success coaching players on the PGA Tour. When I began working as a clinical and sport psychologist, I never thought I would suffer from the ongoing impact of anxiety. I dreamt of my career for so long, and part of it was that I would not have to stress about my clients.

I did not pursue a full-time role in clinical settings because of my anxiety. I feared that I would not be of assistance to those who were suffering and that I would eventually make them worse. I would worry over weekends about clients who were severely depressed, praying they would make it through the weekend. Instead of doing clinical work, I worked in the pharmaceutical sector for eight years and was very successful there. But I needed more and a more significant challenge.

When I opened The MindSide, I used to tell my colleagues that I was only going to focus on the performance of athletes. No clinical work would be on my schedule; in theory, this made me feel better.

I thought my most significant worries would be my players playing poorly, not their overall health. I was okay for some time, well, at least until the status of my players increased. Before I knew it, I worked with some of the top players in the world.

As a relative newcomer, I started to experience the same crippling anxieties I had while doing clinical work. This time, it was not my client's overall mental well-being but my obsession with doing a great job. I began to fear being fired!

What I wanted so badly was creating so much stress in my life. I was in a twisted misery of suffering myself, worried that I would get fired if they played poorly, embarrass myself to my colleagues, and worse, I had the worst imposter syndrome possible.

In my first PGA Tour experience, I found myself walking down the fairway of a major, listening to my player and one of his buddies talk about the stresses of playing on Tour. The fact that they were back-to-back major champions did not cause me more anxiety; the sheer fact that I was on the PGA Tour gave me tremendous pressure.

How did being on Tour give me such anxiety, especially when I had dreamt of being there for so long?

I wanted to work with the best players in the world, but now that I was there, why was I so nervous?

I texted my wife and shared how stressed out I was, and she texted me back, "Well, you may only be there once, so give it everything you have!" It made sense and was a logical response. Rationally, she was right. But I was still a nervous wreck.

I felt like a complete imposter, trying to do the work as I thought a "real" psychologist should, not focused on what the client needed. I used the traditional cliques in the mental game, like "you just have to stay present," "one shot at a time," and other mental diarrhea. When she texted me back, I thought, "screw it. They will get everything I have."

I went for it. I don't know if it worked, though. The player who brought me in that week would connect here or there for a year or so, but several years later, he eventually hired me to join his team. We ended up working together for seven years.

But I remained a nervous ball of energy. I dreaded going out on Tour each week, feeling doom on the flight out to the city and an intoxicating sense of relief when I boarded my return flight home.

Working as a psychologist on Tour was a dream job, yet I was in complete emotional turmoil, and I worried more about my players' suffering than succeeding. The crazy thing is that since I started working on Tour, my players have won over 25 Tour events, several majors, and many more worldwide. They were killing it, and I was eating myself inside out.

And yes, I have been fired. Each time, I replaced the player with a better player.

How did something I love cause so much pain inside me?

Why would something I was pretty good at cause me so much misery?

Would this ever stop, and could I "enjoy" my work?

Those Damn Doubts

Everyone has doubts. The bigger the moment, the more consequences are involved and the higher the energy, which guarantees you will have more doubts. Why do you have doubts? If you are prepared, why would doubts even show up?

I have read repeatedly that preparation and belief guarantee a rock-solid mindset.

Wrong.

That perspective sells many books but fails you because it does not showcase the reality that doubts are present for a singular purpose – to draw attention to your insecurities so you can either overcome them or improve them.

Here are some of the most common doubts that I find drive anxiety:

Self-Doubt – Can I succeed? Am I good enough to do this? Do I have the tools to be good enough?

All fair questions. Each question has an element of truth that can create significant difficulty for you. What if you fail, and how will you even know if you will succeed? How do you respond?

To remedy these doubts, it comes back to your OPM and trusting that your mindset will align you with the energy and tools to face the challenge. Success will always be uncertain and unknown, so you must improve your processes without guaranteeing success.

Doubt – Can I Get Better?

Training requires significant sacrifices, and it is natural to want to see a return on your investments, and it would suck to do all that work and not improve.

You are never a finished product. Your performance levels in sports and life will improve in a different timeframe than you want. That is simply the price of admission in the competitive arena. If you worry you are not improving, your doubts and anxiety will spike. Instead of limiting yourself to what you think the top level of your performance should be, focus on the journey and the wisdom you gain along the way. See growth, not validation.

Doubt – Why Is This Not Happening Faster?

Patience is so hard, particularly in today's world of immediate results. With rising demands and the power of perfectionism, it is hard to trust the process if you are not experiencing results fast enough.

Success takes time, much longer than you anticipated. Be careful of overnight successes because the processes used to obtain short-term success are not built for longevity.

You must be patient and work to improve the processes driving your results, regardless of the immediate results. The most considerable risk is when you fail to see your progress because you are so focused on the drama of the current challenge. It is hard to have a healthy perspective when you are so focused on the immediate struggles that you forget your past triumphs.

Shift your perspective to learning instead of eliminating struggle. Growth takes longer than the mind wants, and you rarely remember your past victories. Focus on those victories to slow your impatience and doubts down.

Doubt - Coaching/Leadership

Great coaching will expose your doubts if done with a system or process guiding it. That does not mean it will be easy for you to accept. I don't know if the coaching or leadership you have in your life right now is right for you, but it is *the one* you have right now. The goal is to learn to navigate the challenging moments and demanding leadership and not resist the opportunity to learn something from the environment. One may ask about unhealthy or abusive coaching relationships, which require a different action. Eventually, you must remove yourself from that environment, but not every challenging coaching relationship is abusive. Some of the greatest teachers I ever had were my most difficult experiences.

Doubt - Is this System Right for Me?

According to the NCAA website, nearly 16,000 college athletes entered the transfer portal in 2020 and 2021 combined. Of those who entered the transfer portal, only 49% found a new destination. Does the data suggest that players cannot handle the systems of their original schools or other factors involved? If slightly less than half found a new destination, what drives the desire to leave?

No system is ideal at the start because you must learn what your role is. Instead of looking for simplicity or ease, look for how to learn to become a part of the system. Do not fight it because it is hard or you fear it. Face the doubt telling you that the system does not work for you by shifting the question to how you can take elements of the system and experience and make it work for you.

Doubt – I Shouldn't Be Feeling This!

Emotional confusion is common, and so is judging what you are feeling. The problem is that few people disclose what they emotionally experience to others. In fact, wouldn't it be easier if we could see a thought bubble above everyone's heads? It would be so much easier to see someone's doubts, another's insecurities, and still, another's anxieties. That would also help me feel better about my thoughts, fears, and doubts!

What you feel is authentic and unique to you. Instead of questioning it, learn to investigate it to learn more. Your emotions are not about WHY but WHAT.

Doubt – I Don't Think I Can Do This

You may fail. Failure must always be an option.

What is the worst thing that can happen?

Fail?

Struggle?

Have people questioned your ability?

Instead of worrying about a future you cannot control and struggling to succeed because you are afraid of failing, shift your mindset towards getting better.

Instead of asking if you can succeed, how about you change your perspective and challenge yourself to see what you can achieve? There are so many strategies you can learn to face the different challenges in your life, but instead of seeing the doubts as definitive, see them as developmental invitations.

Doubts are not a problem and should not perceived as dangerous. You must change your perspective. The truth is that my perspective changed, and that has helped me. I still have significant doubts and painful anxiety, and sometimes I worry more after my players win than when they struggle, but I have a better mindset about my work than I did in the past

6

YOU GOT THIS!

Scott was terrified of going through his first fall camp in college. As a highly recruited player, he had the physical tools to compete, but he had never been in an environment where he was pushed, coached, and trained now that he was on campus.

Fall camp can be brutal. The summer temperatures can push 95 degrees, and with the humidity in the south, the heat index can easily eclipse 100 degrees. Back then, few considerations existed for a player's physical health during the hot training days. Coaches would see players who passed out from the heat, vomited, or needed water as "weak-minded."

Training sessions today are so much more structured and monitored. Athletic trainers constantly monitor players' body temperatures, utilizing numerous technological innovations to cool them off rapidly. Biometric data gets collected as do "effort" assessments, calculating exertion loads, speed, endurance, and other related outputs. Players cannot simply coast in training now.

Even though there is more support now, summer training is still hard. Summer training is more of a mind game than anything else. The two hours on the field can feel like an eternity, with moments of challenge mixed with learning stations.

All athletes dread fall camp. The long hours, physical exhaustion, and endless practices eventually wear down the most mentally balanced athletes. Scott did not just dread it but feared it. The novelty was overwhelming and triggered significant doubts and insecurities.

"What will they see in me if I can't make it through practice?"

"If I can't do it this year, how will I ever play here?"

His doubts grew with each doubt. As his anxiety grew, so did his physical pains. Suddenly, he struggled with his hamstring. In the middle of practice, he would feel a strain in his hamstring and must pull himself out of practice. He would retreat to the training room.

There was solace in the training room and support, attention, and even the ability to find confidence there. When Scott couldn't return to practice, he felt more confident that he could endure the heat and training. As soon as the athletic trainers cleared him to return, he would feel the crush of doubt again.

He did not believe he could succeed. Why would he? He had never been through a brutal fall camp, and everyone kept telling him to prepare for the challenges, even the ones he didn't know.

I had him lay out all the scenarios – what would happen should he fail? Where would he go if he had to transfer? What would happen if he missed the year because of his hamstring?

He lacked confidence and self-belief. It was not the doubts that were the problem.

He feared the unknown; the only thing he knew about it was that it was brutal. When you are experiencing high anxiety, your mind is in a blender.

Why focus on things in the future that you cannot control at the expense of things you know? Scott focused all his energy on what could happen in those miserable fall camps and ignored that he could face anything.

Scott and I worked on knowing what he knew, not fearing what he did not know.

When facing difficult circumstances, competitors like Scott romanticize perfect competitive outcomes as the measure of success, and those are truly unrealistic. Confidence takes a hit as the *perfect* outcomes become more difficult in those hard training sessions. Instead of seeing endurance, grittiness, and resiliency as the goal, perfection becomes the only outcome worthy of a "passing grade." Skills that can be developed in those circumstances get overlooked for superficial outcomes – make it through it instead of using the challenge to get better.

You do the same thing.

Scott ignored that he could endure, face, and overcome any challenge. Every one of us is a successful failure; lacking in those situations is the depth of your mental toolkit.

Scott had to learn what to do when those doubts picked up thinking about practice. Remember, your thoughts ultimately rise from your innermost insecurities, so you will only see the worst-case scenarios when you have negative thoughts and doubts like Scott. You completely ignore your capabilities.

Scott could endure the significant physical and mental demands and dominate at practice. The problem was that he didn't believe he could endure the insecurities of failing in competition. The closer he got to the competition, the faster he wanted to escape. His "injured" hamstring became a great tool to get a "get out of difficulty" pass.

Once Scott changed his mindset towards believing that he could endure any challenge, he started to see a growth in his confidence. For too long, he erroneously believed there would be a day when training should become easy.

Growing up, Scott had been told that prepared athletes do not feel insecure, do not let the doubts in, and take struggles and build success.

Every motivational or inspirational message seemed to glorify the toughness rather than the endurance that built the toughness.

Once he abandoned the idea that the struggle was a sign of falling behind and embraced growth through struggle, he became a warrior throughout camp.

His level of play remains high, and his success continues.

Scott changed his mindset and shifted his focus to a shorter-term lens. It was no longer about what tomorrow's practice would be. Instead, I got him to believe that the uncertainty of tomorrow was nothing but a mirage of the unknown and instead of realizing that he needed to focus on the moment because looking forward was destroying him.

There was nothing he was going through that he could not endure. He had the physical ability and the competitive mindset. While it was hard to get him to believe in the true potential of his abilities, I knew if he focused on the singular moment and his readiness to compete, then he could endure right now and dominate it.

Stop looking at how far you must go and start looking at how far you have come – despite your anxiety.

You will have doubts, fears, and anxieties. They do not predict if you will be successful; instead, they remind you of the challenge in front of you.

Nothing can predict success, but developing your tools and skills will increase those odds of success. Each time you face a challenge and reframe or refocus at the moment, your tools improve, even if you struggle. Success cannot mean the absence of struggle or discomfort; anxiety is the invitation to the present, not the prediction of the future.

The nature of anxiety is that it shifts your perspective towards a romantic life without anxiety, believing that you can only succeed when you are without the pains of worry, stress, and the general struggles of life.

Anxiety hijacks your pride, trying to convince you to be ashamed of what you are experiencing and fearful of the future because of your discomfort.

Success is uncomfortable, brutal, and unrelenting. Anxiety changes the way you think about the future and, in doing so, shifts your lens on how you see your circumstances.

Anxiety does not accurately predict or reflect anything wrong, as anxiety is just raising your awareness of things outside your immediate control.

The following chapters will help you shift your lens and realize that beating the crap out of anxiety happens when you know that anxiety will no longer stop your progress or production. You will always have it.

I still experience anxiety and worry when trapped by pressures, responsibilities, and life demands. Sometimes, it hits me right before I go on stage to give a talk in front of thousands or when I am on a flight with turbulence.

I have learned that the presence of my anxiety is not a problem, so instead, I embrace the feelings, welcoming the discomfort because the sheer fact invites me to get fully invested in the moment.

7

ENTER THE RING WITH THE MINDSET
OF AUTHORITY

Mike Tyson paced the ring.

Michael Spinks paced his corner of the ring.

Two undefeated heavyweight champions readied themselves for a prize fight in front of tens of thousands of a live audience and millions on pay-per-view. I was one of those people who paid for pay-per-view.

I loved Mike Tyson in his prime. He carried himself with such intensity that it often sparked fear in his opponents.

Spinks was no slouch. He was the middleweight boxing gold medalist in the 1976 Olympic Games in Montreal, Canada. Entering the fight, Spinks was 31-0 as a professional with 21 wins by knockout, and he was considered the heavyweight champion by The Ring and Boxing Illustrated magazines.

As Spinks stood in the ring, fear overtook him, which was evident to anyone watching the fight. His body language showed a competitor uncomfortable at the moment, shifting his eyes, shoulders slumped, and not wanting to be there. If there were an escape door, Spinks would have taken it the minute he saw Tyson approaching the ring.

Tyson was all business. Tyson held the heavyweight champion belts of all boxing sanctioning organizations and was 34-0, with 30 victories by knockout. While smaller than Spinks, Tyson was more powerful and had a reputation for not just beating his opponents but also destroying them.

As Tyson moved around the ring, he resembled a caged tiger, ready to pounce. His movements were not protective; instead, he looked primed for a battle, but one on his terms. He stood by himself but did not need anything from his team.

Tyson was ready to fight. Spinks was not.

When the opening bell rang, Tyson attacked. He launched an unrelenting onslaught of hooks, catching Spinks in the first ten seconds with a stunning left hook that forced Spinks to cover up. Tyson kept attacking, eventually causing Spinks to take a knee from a right hand to the body, putting him on the mat for the first time just seconds into the fight.

After the standing count, Spinks came into Tyson, missing with a right hand, but Tyson countered with a crushing combination, knocking Spinks out. It was a powerful piece of sports imagery, as cameras showed Spinks laying flat on his back, with the lowest ropes forced to the mat and eyes rolled back in his head.

Night-night!!

Destruction in ninety-one seconds.

I ordered this fight on Pay-per-View. If I remember correctly, it cost around $50. I was ready to watch the fight that night, and it was over before it started. Tyson dominated from the opening bell.

Spinks later said that fear was taking him over in the fight. Tyson had a plan, but evidently, Spinks was looking for an escape.

Tyson had to feel something leading into the fight, too. According to media reports, Spinks' team had accused Tyson of padding his gloves in the pre-fight inspection, and the groundless accusation angered Tyson.

How does one fighter use the anger for motivation, and the other get overwhelmed by the arousal, becoming scared in the biggest moment, right before a championship bout?

Tyson showed up with purpose. The sudden adrenaline rush focused Tyson, and he didn't see that energy as a negative; instead, he morphed it into his game plan.

You will always have arousal, adrenaline, anxiety, and even anger, and those feelings will always be with you. What is critical is that you understand that the simple presence of those different experiences is nothing more than your body responding to uncertainty, challenges, and threats, real and imagined.

You do not control what you think or feel, but you can influence your actions despite what you feel.

Anxiety is present. It will not simply go away.

But you must ask yourself – are you Tyson or Spinks in the face of your building anxiety?

Anxiety is not the defining nature of who you are.

You are more complex and dynamic than the fears, doubts, and insecurities that attempt to define your existence. It feels like anxiety wants to take your mind over and appear impossible, but the only way is through it.

Setting a game plan by shifting your mental perspective will create the momentum to build confidence and push you towards a better future. The harder you attempt to resist the anxiety, avoid it, or even slash it, the more powerful anxiety controls your entire experience.

You must accept that anxiety will be present in your life. The increased energy from anxiety is beneficial, so use it for your benefit.

To kick anxiety's ass, you must be willing to stand up to the fear of what could happen and face the pain and discomfort of anxiety.

Switching the Game

Anxiety makes you feel powerless about the challenges in your life, thoughts, and future. Whether in life or the midst of a competitive journey, the harder you fight against your anxiety, the louder it gets.

Once you realize you are in control of your experiences, you take control of your anxiety. It is like a switch that flips.

Your anxiety does not define or predict your future. You are in control of your experience – 100% of the time.

Anxiety clouds your judgment, perspective, and mental flexibility. The drama associated with anxiety makes you more sensitive to what others say, even those trying to help. It takes supportive gestures and twists them into biting attacks on your character. And with every struggle, your anxiety takes more control.

Understanding that anxiety is an experience, not a death sentence, changes the game. When you are suffering, you are fighting for your mental health life, working to find relief with every moment of the day. Only when you find that the suffering can flow by you, not own you, does it switch, and you take control.

When you can stand up and face the fear of the "what if's of life," accepting the thoughts as mental noise, the physical discomfort as arousal and not debilitating angst, you begin to gain footing against the floods. The power comes when you realize you can face the noise, stand up to the pain, and not back down. That is unreal power.

You will never know what others think about you. You never know the struggles they manage daily. You only see a representation of what you want to see in them.

If you find yourself impressed with something that they seem to do well and that makes you feel insecure about your progress, then their "strength" is likely reflective of your insecurity more than their strength. Their strength is always relative to your perspective.

The moment you realize that the drama is often intensified through your insecurities opens you up to the potential of a future without lasting pain. You do not have to fixate on what you find lacking in your own life, game, or experience. You can focus on things you do well or follow the rabbit hole of insecurity littered with uncertainty, fears, and endless comparisons. The truth is that you can build from "what can I do" instead of getting lost in "what is going to happen?"

Anxiety shifts your experience and perspective. It highlights what *may* be wrong, not what is wrong. Anxiety lives in the margins of reality, trashing the known strengths to focus you on the potential threats in your life. That must switch to the present realities in your immediate perspective. What you are feeling *right now* demands your total attention.

The focus on the immediate moment gives you power over the present.

What is it that you are fearing? Is it in the future or present?

What are you facing immediately right now, and what can you do to face it? You are reading this sentence, and it needs your attention to comprehend the depth of these comments. Your mind does not need you worrying about the next meeting, competition, or conflict. You can face those when they show up, so redirect your mind to this chapter and ask yourself: "Can I be present and comprehend the question of being invested in being present?"

There are no threats that demand your attention away from this section. Learn to take control by choosing what you focus on. Over time, you will improve, your angst will reduce, and you switch to feeling more empowered.

In the next section, I will take you through actionable steps to help you shift your perspective, manage the physical experiences of anxiety, and build a healthy plan forward. Believe it or not, you can do all three *despite* anxiety. That is how you kick anxiety's ass – you win despite it

8

GETTING RIGHT

The simple nature of anxiety creates a complicated mental mess that threatens relief in the face of fear. With every apprehensive thought about the future, trusting yourself to thrive with anxiety becomes harder. Even worse, the nature of anxiety makes you fear that relief is attainable.

I am unsure if that comes from the fact that anxiety lingers below the surface or is due to the complicated nature of anxiety itself. Anxiety is like the warmth emanating from a fire – there is a fine line between feeling good and getting burned. The fire provides warmth but can burn you if you get too close.

Anxiety only limits you if you accept the power of anxiety to disrupt your life. That only comes from feeling powerless mentally, giving in to the pain.

I have always found it crucial to categorize *what* I feel. When my mind is racing and my body gets tense, I struggle to experience each element of anxiety in its individualized sensation. Instead, I merge each sensation into one giant mess.

Anxiety is like my house's alarm system blaring, shrieking that painful ear-piercing horn to wake me up in the middle of the night. At that moment, I fail to look for what set off the alarm. Was it a door ajar, a broken window, or a bad sensor? When that alarm is blaring, I am not thinking clearly. At that moment, I just want the alarm to stop.

You must start to learn what it is for you and how to understand the individual aspects of your anxiety within the entire picture.

As the legendary musician Tom Petty sings in *You Don't Know How It Feels To Be Me,* each experience of life is genuinely personal. The following categorizations and the plan to kick anxiety's ass are not the Gospel but a recipe to individualize your experience.

To start, I want you to conceptualize the experience of anxiety into three buckets: Perspective, Perception, and The Plan.

Perspective

Anxiety changes how you interpret experiences, your potential in the future, and the reason for your angst. Your perspective changes the lens through which you view the world. It is far too easy to get caught up in overly reactive, habitual patterns of seeing the pains of anxiety as the way of the future, that the world is constantly beating you down, and that you are powerless against those challenges. But if you change the lens of your world, you can change your experience.

I will share ideas that will help you shift your perspective to see anxiety differently to take back your life.

Perception

The most powerful aspect of anxiety lies in its ability to dramatically hijack your thoughts and physical sensations. It is not "just in your head." Anxiety lives in every element of you. But it does not have to be in control.

Understanding your physical relationship with anxiety gives you a sense of control. Just because you feel something different or uncomfortable does not mean you must control it.

Wait, how do you control it if you should not control it?

Understanding the power of your perception is appreciating how the energy of anxiety flows through you. Control realizes that you are not powerless but instead starts to use that same energy towards productive expressions of you.

Let me explain a bit more.

As anxiety builds, whether due to a specific event or just in the background, the energy starts pushing against everything you have. Much like a rock rolling down a hill, you will not stop it. You hope to redirect its path towards something else. If you try to stop that rock, it will knock you over. If you nudge it in different directions, its path will slightly shift, and over time, the tumbling rock will dramatically change its path.

Knowing how that energy of anxiety dominates every other experience makes you want to stop it immediately. But that does not work. Having the enhanced perception of increasing anxiety allows you to redirect it, not stop it.

That is a powerful concept to understand. You cannot relax in the middle of an anxiety storm. You cannot ignore it or control it. Once you know it is building, find a place to direct that energy.

The Plan

Is there anything that can happen to you that you cannot create a plan forward? Too much time is spent in sports and life trying to prevent bad things from happening. Why waste time preventing a hypothetical versus facing the immediate moment before you?

No one wants to deal with the negative drama of life. Yet, you are very good at it. You spend too much time obsessing about the future, but you can face whatever it brings, even if it sucks.

You are not paralyzed by anxiety unless you accept the potential dangers of the future will win. You can respond to every challenge by developing a plan to attack the challenge, even if that plan is to determine the nature and severity of the problem.

While I struggle with this personally, I am good at consulting with clients about this very point. I have spent years counseling coaches about the fears of being fired by their organization, only to answer the call after their firing with, "OK, so now what?"

Amazingly, they respond to being fired and losing their job every single time by self-reflection and analysis. The actual event of being fired rapidly changes their disposition, shifting to an attitude of aggressiveness that would have served them brilliantly before getting fired.

It is as if the "What If" creates greater hesitancy and fear than the "What Now?"

Years ago, I had a professional athlete rehabilitating from a significant arm injury. Despite all indications that he was progressing ahead of schedule, he fixated on the risk of reinjury. That fear consumed him. For months, he could not verbalize future pursuits because he was terrified of the risk of reinjury. This fear was not irrational, as it is part of every injury rehabilitation I have ever worked with, but there is not much you can do to avoid it outside of doing your best in your treatment sessions.

Unfortunately, he injured his arm again as he was close to returning to competition. It was the same injury that sidelined him initially. I thought it was going to devastate him.

But it didn't.

"I know what to do, and I knew this would happen. Now, I have a plan," he told me.

It is weird; sometimes, the events we fear the most need to be present front and center to commit fully to the plan we need to follow. The underlying issue was that his plan to face the new injury was what he had been doing for months, so it felt normal for him. He knew how to plan each day and was aware of every challenge that would show up.

You never lose your power to create a plan for a new challenge. Anxiety cannot steal that from you.

Next Steps

In the next section, I will take you through the different aspects of each component – Perspective, Perception, and The Plan.

9

THE POWER IN PERSPECTIVE

Perched on a hilltop overlooking the Portland Harbor sits the Portland Head Light, the iconic lighthouse that has been navigating sailors for over 200 years. Facing the treacherous waters where the Atlantic Ocean meets the coastal waters of North America, this iconic lighthouse serves as the warning sign for the dangerous shoreline, ready to guide them through the volatile weather and the ultimate beacon of the safety of their return home.

Lighthouses have existed since the reported original Pharos of Alexandria in ancient Egypt in 280 BC. While modern technology has changed their mechanisms of action, their presence remains strong today.

Their ultimate purpose is to provide safe passage in dangerous conditions and signal dangerous approaching shorelines in low visibility. Each lighthouse is different and built to maximize visibility in various precarious conditions.

Whether seen through the fog on a cliff or the light-piercing torrential downpours of rain, lighthouses provide the perspective of risk, safety, and pathways to safety. Anxiety is not much different, and you must realize the power of that perspective.

I used to hate the anxiety I felt, wishing I would not be restricted from the freedoms I wanted to have in my professional life. I did not want to worry about my clients or dread week-long trips across the globe at top golf courses. I was angry to live *with* anxiety, not realizing that anxiety was who I was.

Like the lighthouse on that cliff, my anxiety was not the *real* issue. The presence of a lighthouse did not say there was imminent danger, but instead, there could be danger and to be on high alert.

My anxiety was not the issue. My perspective towards it was. And that had to change.

How Did My Perspective Change?

I am about to show you how everything changed for me.

I learned through my reflections that I had been putting too much emphasis on trying to survive and not on things that make me better. My personal growth mattered more than enduring the storms of anxiety. I needed to be more flexible in facing inside and outside challenges.

It has not been an easy transition, as I battle my anxieties daily. I travel to unique places and work with the world's best in their sport. I have become friends with individuals I used to admire, which is a humbling experience.

I will take you through the powerful mental shift that helped me move from a person of fear to one of empowerment. From this point forward in the book, I will help you kick anxiety's ass. The pain of anxiety will not go away, but you will fight it every day and win the battle every chance you have in every moment.

It starts with the mindset shift about anxiety, not changing you. Shifting your perspective requires you to be flexible to the moment, what you are feeling, and what you think you *should* be feeling.

Over the past several decades, psychological or mental flexibility has garnered significant attention in treatment circles. Whether we call it psychological flexibility, as Dr. Hayes referenced and Dr. Todd Kasdin conceptualized in his academic article in 2010 in *Clinical Psychology Reviews* (for the science geeks who want to read more on Dr. Kasdin, check out his article Kasdin, TB (2010). Psychological Flexibility as a Fundamental Aspect of Health. *Clin Psych Rev,* 30(7), 865-78) or see it from Dr. David's perspective as emotional agility, the concept is critical to shifting your perspective in the face of anxiety. Despite what I feel, I can experience anything by adapting to the possibilities instead of becoming imprisoned by the pain of the moment.

Through all the different writings, mental or psychological flexibility focuses on what you do *with* the experience and how to move forward *despite* what you feel, what is happening, or what conflicts stand in the way.

There are definite elements of mindfulness, to be not judgmental of what you are feeling and not make negative assumptions about yourself because of what you are feeling. Changing your perspective requires flexibility away from the chains of negative judgments about yourself simply because of how you feel or what you are experiencing.

If you can change your perspective to see what is possible, NO MATTER what you feel, you can adapt to anything. It starts with that!

Being mentally flexible requires you to understand that you cannot always change what is happening to you, but you can always find an appropriate direction. Success may require you to see things differently, to make a change in your behavior, or to prepare for additional challenges. To be flexible means you can bend but not break.

You can always find a way through the troubles of the moment, adapt to the circumstances, and ultimately learn from those lessons. If you can be present, you can find a way, any way, forward.

Anxiety wants you to believe the future is scary and that success is unlikely. Mental flexibility allows you to be anxious but still find a way to be successful. You must become aware of what is happening and accept that it is out of your control, but then find your stability in the storm and push forward.

Perspective is the start of putting anxiety in its place. The presence of discomfort does not predict the future. Unfortunately, too often, anxiety triggers resistance, resentment, and frustration, only causing more problems.

You must see anxiety in a different light. You are not at a disadvantage because you have anxiety. Not unless you buy into that fear.

What is anxiety preventing you from doing?

Competing without freedom?

Feeling calm and comfortable?

Speaking in public?

Believing in yourself?

Anxiety is not preventing you. You are preventing yourself from progressing *with* anxiety because you are fighting the presence *of* anxiety. You do not want to suffer and do not want to have to deal with anxiety's bullshit.

I know that because that was me. I was so pissed, but I had to learn to change my perspective toward everything associated with anxiety and begin to accept that I could do everything with anxiety that I wanted to do without it. Living *with* anxiety will never stop me from progressing.

10

THE POWER OF ACCEPTANCE

I sat across the room from my therapist, a local psychologist who I have worked with to help me deal with the stresses of life and the anxiety that is always percolating.

"Bhrett, you work so hard to change what you feel. You rationalize it to me, describe it differently, and immediately switch your train of thought to the next moment. You seem to struggle with simply being okay with where you are."

Oomph. Right in the jaw. She was right. I needed to hear that.

Acceptance is being so present-focused, so immersed in the feelings of *right now* that the "what if" no longer matters. Acceptance is becoming great at observing life but not changing the experience. The lighthouse from the last chapter is just a lighthouse. The function of a lighthouse makes it valuable, not the structure itself.

Anxiety has a function. It really does.

Stop Fighting Your Relationship with Anxiety

The pressure to conform to society's standards does nothing but rob greatness from the diversity of life. When competing in life, your perspective is as unique as your genetic code. Sure, there are traits of the greats to study, but never abandon who you are for the desires of another to make you fit into a specific box.

The harder you try to rewrite who you are, the faster you abandon your natural talents. Success often favors the early developers throughout sports, only to fall behind those who mature later. Unfortunately, many potential superstars likely quit the game, overlooked by coaches, parents, and colleagues who convince those later bloomers they are not good enough.

I was one of those late bloomers. I played one year of varsity baseball, took four years to play in college, and did not shave every day until I had graduated college. Thankfully, I had people believe in me – my parents, college coach, and some family friends.

Today, I don't know if how I conduct my professional work is congruent with society's demands, but I embrace my individuality more than in the past. I like to wear shorts, so I wear shorts. I cuss, so I let it rip. I study by watching YouTube videos more than reading, so I share videos with my clients.

I do not want you to order my dinner, and I won't order yours. I want to eat what feeds me, not what you think I should eat.

Who will tell you lived an extraordinary life when you lie on your deathbed? Those random individuals who told you that you were doing things wrong or those you positively impacted?

When your life ends, you retire from your profession, or you decide to walk away from competition, the only thing that matters is the investment you made into your life, craft, or those you serve.

The critics will not be there.

I have not met many athletes who retire who wished they would not have given so much to their sport. I don't know many who wanted to listen to more critics.

The presence of difficulty does not diminish the value of your accomplishments. No one said it would be easy. You must learn to start accepting who you are and learn to value your own opinion of yourself.

You will make mistakes, and even some may be regrettable. That does not mean that you cannot make a difference right now. Life and competition are about investing in the present moment, not validating what you think you should be or rewriting your past. Accept where you are right now and get better.

I get tired of coaches telling me to change a player's personality so they can fit into a team better. Why does a coach know more about a player's personality than the player? Could they be a better teammate? Sure. The self-improvement industry spends way too much time trying to change people than embracing the nature of individuality.

If a player gets nervous before a game, is that bad? No.

Is that bad if a player likes to be quiet, reserved, and alone? No.

Is that bad if a player is loud, boisterous, and even agitated? No.

My question is always this: "Could it be beneficial?" There are variances across every continuum in life. Some days, you are anxious and play great, but others, you are anxious and play terribly. So what. Stop trying to predict the future, change your feelings, or be different. Start accepting your psychological fingerprint, and you more effectively meet the demands now.

Be who you are. Embrace your uniqueness and your perspectives.

You are always in development, and your perspective will grow as you experience new challenges. You will gain wisdom through learning and find new ways to face struggles.

Anxiety tells you that you are not good enough for the future. Learn to accept that you are exactly who needs to face your future. You will continually improve if you face the future with the unrestricted nature of who you are, learn from each moment, and then push forward again toward the following outcome.

If you are committed to changing who you are, you will feel forced to abandon every strength you have. Instead, I want you to embrace your psychological fingerprint and everything that comes with that. I want you to start spending the energy you have wasted trying to change yourself and using it to invest in yourself. Now is the time to accept you for who you are, how you are, and that you are constantly growing.

Acceptance is About Accepting Who You Are with What is Happening to You

I was standing on the practice tee during The Open Championship in St. Andrews, Scotland, talking to a few of my players and their coaches about their expectations of the tournament for the upcoming week when a thought about anxiety hit me. The wind was blowing straight into us on the driving range, and it was cold, a bit wet, and a pure reminder of the elements that make The Open Championship one of the most challenging tournaments of the year. My mind was all over the place, thinking about what my players needed to do to prepare for the championship week.

With the wind blowing 40 miles per hour, the players had to prepare to flight the golf ball to pierce the wind. There are so many yardage calculations and strategic decisions that the players and their caddies must commit to that any indecision could have tragic results. I asked the coaches how they adjust their information for those types of weeks and what adjustments they make to help their players.

"It depends on the player," one of my coaches said. This coach is highly respected, highly accomplished, and a coach who speaks very few words. His players have had tremendous success, and he has taken multiple players to Major championship victories over the years.

"It always depends on what they want to do with the ball because I can tell them, but if it does not match what they want, then I am wasting my time."

That information was not groundbreaking or something I had yet to hear before. When coaching the world's best athletes, they are the world's best for a reason. They see shots, know the game from the "insider's perspective," and have thousands more high-pressure hours than I could ever have. I always want my players to verbalize what they are feeling and experiencing so I can understand their personal experiences of competitive moments.

The conversation continued, and the other coaches provided support for their individualized coaching methods. One of my players asked another player, "Do you do that journaling that Doc has me do? It helps me so much." The other player looked at me and asked, "We haven't talked about that, have we?"

I answered quickly. "No. He (the other player) has to have a way to download his training, competitive rounds, and mental state to help him move on. You move on immediately, and I get the downloads from your caddy. Journaling will cause you an additional burden, not help at all."

While journaling helps, there is a small subset of individuals that I have found struggle with journaling because it creates more stress than helps. This world-class player was one of those. This exchange led to a follow-up discussion among the coaches, players, and caddies on the range about how everyone sees the course, the conditions, and the tournament differently.

I asked them to verbalize a shot to one of the flags on the left side of the range, with the 40-mile-a-hour wind having shifted from the left side of the range, blowing straight across the range towards the right. Each person on the range described the wind, trajectory, flight, and result differently.

One player described the technical approach. Another described it visually. And another from a feel.

Each player and caddie described it in their terms. The descriptions got complicated when they tried to get someone else to understand their perspective.

It reminded me of a **Golf Channel** show with Tiger Woods and Anthony Kim years ago. At the time, Woods was dominating at every level. Kim was a new arrival to the world scene, bringing a different style to the game. Kim was creative, different, and nontraditional. Unfortunately, a wrist injury ended Kim's career, and he has drifted into folklore, like a mythical wizard who returned to the mountains only to be spoken of due to their past magical exploits.

As Woods led the clinic, an audience member asked, "How do you hit a cut shot?"

Woods took the audience into a rather specific and in-depth discussion on the physics of the golf swing, how he practices the shot, and how to execute under pressure. As the greatest player to ever play the game, Woods made a complicated discussion seem relatively easy.

He then asked Kim how he hit a cut shot. Kim walked up to the hitting station, looked at the audience, and said, "I just see it."

And he fired a perfect cut into the driving range. Woods just shook his head and laughed.

As a psychologist, I know the importance of the individual's expression of personality, expectations, and stress. As a coach, I work hard to emphasize that, but it is nice to be reminded as I was on that driving range at The Open Championship.

Every player has their own perspective. It is as unique as their fingerprint.

Your Psychological Fingerprint

There are over eight billion people on this planet. Eight billion different expressions of life.

There are thousands of shades of blue and a million combinations of building the perfect hamburger. If you think your perspective needs to change to become more like another person, you are ignoring your unique interactions with life.

Why do you try to emulate anyone else when your perspective is unique?

One of the elements of humanity that makes it so fantastic is there are no two individuals alike. My mother was an identical twin, and she and her sister differed. They looked identical and had similar mannerisms, but they viewed the world differently. Neither was right or wrong, just different.

You are unique in your own right. Your genetic code, background, and experiences influence your skills, abilities, and talents. You also have superpowers, those skills, and elite talents.

Everyone has their superpowers.

However, too much focus is on physical skills and talents, and more attention should be paid to those mental skills.

Too many people abandon their standing in who they are, trying to become something they think other people want them to become.

Do not do that. You are who you are, years in the making.

Every experience you have encountered has formed the situation you are in now and, more importantly, built the tools to face those challenges.

You will develop more tools, but the ingredients are in place. You are not broken. Be you.

Your psychological fingerprint forms who you are, your personality, and how you face challenges.

What is the worst that can happen?

Get back up, face the next challenge, and get to work. That is the same thing as if you had success.

Your psychological fingerprint is more significant than any result.

It is not motivation but reality. You are completely capable of facing every challenge before you.

You can face it.

Anxiety tells you that you cannot survive the challenge, which is bullshit. Your psychological fingerprint deserves to be challenged, not protected.

ace the challenge and the storm that may be out there?

Of course.

The doubts and fears will always be there, but you can create a stronger, more resilient competitor in the face of whatever you face.

It is essential to learn who you are. Listen to the world around you.

Imagine yourself 30 years from now. Why wouldn't you want to become better, grind, face challenges, and deal with your difficulties so long as it contributes to a better version of yourself?

You are always a work in progress. See the power of progress.

Who Are You?

Learn to find out. Every challenge you experience forces your mind to ask you questions about who you are. Who you are today is more developed than five years ago.

You are not disadvantaged because others seem to have it more manageable. By focusing on their successes, you ignore their trials and tribulations. Focus on building a better version of yourself.

In the heat of the moment, your psychological fingerprint will emerge. You must simplify the engagement, and everything else is noise.

Are you a Ferrari or a work truck? Both vehicles have benefits, but both can struggle in the wrong situation. You wouldn't use a Ferrari to tow a heavy load, and you wouldn't use a work truck for racing a Grind Prix.

If you are naturally introverted, you do not have to learn to become the life of the party.

It is not who you are.

If you are anxious, it is okay. You probably cannot become a "carefree" player, whatever that is.

Your anxiety does work for you. Stop fighting it and start realizing that it is there for a positive reason you feel the way you do.

Stop trying to be other people. It is a complete waste of time.

Your anxiety drives your insecurities, and vice versa. Everyone has insecurities.

Having insecurities is part of being human and is beneficial to your development. You would not strive to get better if you didn't have insecurities.

When you are anxious, you fixate on your insecurities. They are no longer areas of improvement but rather become reasons for continued failure. You become fixated on what other competitors do well, locking into their strengths and obsessing about your shortcomings. You fixate on their strengths because they match your limitations, driving a more significant gap into what you perceive as a weakness. That is anxiety driving those comparisons.

It doesn't matter what other people do as a measuring stick for what you do. You must own your journey. You have special skills that others do not have. There are parts of you that others recognize in you, but you don't know that.

Your psychological fingerprint is what makes you who you are. Comparison is nothing more than wasted energy and will not get you where you want to be. You might as well piss in your cereal.

Here are a few questions for you about accepting who you are and what you are feeling in your life:

- Does what you are feeling prevent you from what you want to accomplish?

- If yes, why? If you want to play at the top level but are afraid you may fail, imagine if you learned to face that fear and realized it might make you better.

- Have you ever had success feeling amped up, stressed, or tense? I bet you have.

- Would you be more or less successful if you had no anxiety? I bet you would say more, but is that a given? Do you know for certain, or are you just assuming?

My point is this: stop fighting against who you are. You have anxiety. So, what? Who cares if you have anxiety? Trust me; you can manage, succeed, and continue to grow *with* anxiety.

I know you can. The choice is yours.

I never said it would be easy, comfortable, or rewarding. So do not wish for something you don't know, just hoping to eliminate what you do know. That is the power of acceptance.

11

STOP RUNNING FROM ANXIETY – FACE IT!

The pressure to perform perfectly drives the unfortunate urge to find shortcuts when struggling. Instead of working through the struggles, the anxious mind searches for the escape route at the first sign of the problem.

Avoidance becomes the goal, not achievement.

The one thing that we need help with is that we don't see growth as the standard. In today's desire for quick success, whatever the underlying motivation, the presence of struggle can be perceived as not good enough, no matter how much training or improvement you attain.

You have the right to improve. You do not have to be great today so long as you work towards the best version of yourself. And that is always under construction.

This mindset shifts your perspective, not to avoid the discomfort you are feeling but to face the struggle and push through it. When relief from your pain is your motivation, those pains will continue to build.

Anxiety that is avoided becomes the bully in your life.

Face the Bully In Your Mind

Bullies exert dominance because they make you insecure about your thoughts and actions. Bullies stay on the offensive constantly, making you worry when they show up, how they will torture you, and if the pain will ever end.

The more you want them to leave you alone, the more they come after you. Instead of realizing what you can do to defeat the bully, your mind wants to escape the pain and find relief with all its attention.

Scott Farkus cannot define your experience.

Anxiety is the bully in the elementary school playground.

Anxiety is Scott Farkus.

In the cult holiday classic, *A Christmas Story*, the lead character, Ralphie, wants his Red Rider BB Gun for Christmas more than anything.

Throughout the movie, the viewer sees Ralphie's desire to get this special gift from Santa, becoming so consumed that he writes his school paper on how his life will change with the gun. The main arc of the movie is about this desire.

But in the background, Ralphie must deal with a bully. The bully, Scott Farkus, is a seemingly older, red-headed, tough teenager who torments Ralphie, his brother, and friends on the playground and when they walk to school. Since Farkus is bigger than others his age, his tough demeanor terrifies the other kids, resulting in fear and worry every time he shows up.

While the movie did not achieve significant box office success, it became a cult classic due to its frequent showings on cable television over the holiday. I think it resonates with the audience because of the desire for that special Christmas gift, but I believe the bully's presence is critical.

You want something so bad in your pursuits, but the presence of your anxiety is nothing more than a hassle, one that can cause significant impairment. Anxiety is the bully in the playground, interrupting your desires, goals, and aspirations, and it consumes you, sparking great fear the minute it shows up.

The only way to get over it is to give it the Scott Farkus treatment – you must face it and beat the crap out of it. Bullies are tough guys but insecure to their core. So is anxiety.

Anxiety is scary on the surface and gives you every reason to fear what it does to you.

Anxiety tells you that you are not good enough.

Anxiety reminds you of your past struggles.

Anxiety is discomfortable – Is that a word? Anxiety is not uncomfortable. That is the lack of comfort. Discomfort is anxiety. It hurts.

You must face your anxiety: every lie, every fear, and every pain. The more you suppress it, the louder it gets. Anxiety will not simply go away. Anxiety doesn't work like that.

The more you avoid anxiety, like those bullies, the louder the anxiety returns.

You will experience anxiety for life. Sure, some are circumstantial, but what drives anxiety is with you. That is OK. The exact process that drives your results will help you overcome your challenges. Just realize that both processes are fueled by anxiety.

You must face your greatest fears. You must face your anxiety. You must kick its ass to put it in its place. Do not become infatuated with avoiding your fears and the immediate relief from avoidance. The desire for relief creates a dangerous cycle.

Stand Up to Your Fears

What is the worst that can happen? Do not be afraid of that question.

When I get calls from my players about their anxieties, I ask them what they are experiencing. I want to know the physical and mental experiences. Almost immediately, they rattle off a list of dire consequences their poor play could create. They rarely describe what they are experiencing, only future outcomes out of their control.

Anxiety gets you so locked into future threats that you overlook the immediate experience that fuels your growth. While the heat of competition is often discomfortable, it fuels progress. You must use the discomfort as fuel to face your improvement.

When the fear of the moment intensifies, instead of looking down the road and obsessing about every bad outcome, ask yourself, "Can I face what I am feeling?"

Anxiety separates you from the moment with such intensity that you will feel every negative emotion of the past and dread everything in the future. In doing so, you overwhelm your mind with contingency plans, try to rewrite or not repeat your history, and forget to be with what you are currently feeling.

Facing what you feel is critical. I learned that simply describing my feelings during a panic attack allowed me to actively observe the anxiety instead of trying to escape the misery. By paying attention and listening to my body rage in a fire of anxiety, I started to gain control. I gained control by studying the moment and not judging myself in the moment.

So, what if I puke on an airplane? I never have, but I am knocking on the wood of this desk right now.

So, what, right?

Who cares if your playing competitors can see your hands shaking? Do you think they see that as an advantage? Of course not!

Your competitors are too worried about themselves to worry about you. They are probably fighting their shaky hands, too.

No one can see your thoughts, so why do you worry so much about the negative thoughts driving your doubts and insecurity?

Is it because you believed that the best competitors never doubted themselves for so long? Those pesky YouTube videos make you think you should love your journey, quickly overcome struggles, and emerge from victory to a roaring crowd chanting your name.

Let me know when the Tooth Fairy comes back, too.

Stop escaping into your dreams and desires, and instead, work through the struggles that you feel. You will have doubts, insecurities, and negative thoughts. Your mind will drift in competition, and your heart will race.

Anxiety only gets defeated by standing up to it.

To beat anxiety, it must be a front-and-center experience – FACE it!

The Principal's Office

I received a text message one day from one of my professional athletes. The text was my worst nightmare. It read, "Doc, do you have five minutes tomorrow to talk?" Oh shit.

When I get messages like that, it feels like I am sitting in one of the three wooden chairs that always seem to be sitting outside of a principal's office in school. I swear those chairs were wired for pain, tapping into your psyche and filling it with worry and apprehension.

Each chair carried the pains of every student who had ever sat there. They were the cast iron pans of chairs.

I worried all night about that text message. I struggle with ambiguity because uncertainty drives up my anxiety, and I think I have let down my client.

I struggle with FOFU – Fear of Fucking Up. I never want to let down someone who trusted me. When I get a text message like that, I immediately think I have let them down and run through every scenario where I felt I failed. Trust me - I can find a zillion reasons.

The next day, I was traveling and had an early morning flight. I had no problem waking up to my alarm as I thought I had slept, ready to go, because I was so anxious that I sweated out every ounce of fluid in my body. When my plane landed, I texted my player and said, "Give me 10 minutes, and I will find a quiet place to call you." He replied, "Sounds good."

Come on! Tell me more! What did I do?

With my sweaty palms struggling to hold the phone, I called my player, tucked away in the corner of a dead hallway in the airport.

I was stressed because I hate being fired, but to me, it is more that I let them down.

As my player started talking, I waited for the guillotine to fall on my neck and couldn't listen to what he had to say. I was hoping it would be quick and painless.

I told myself I would do what I always do in those situations – be gracious, tell them they can always come back, and thank them for the opportunity. Be a bigger man, right?

My player said, "Look, I only need five minutes to tell you 'thank you for your help.' I have seen such improvement over the past three events. I am excited about the future and just wanted you to know."

Shit – I survived! I didn't even listen to the words at first. I was waiting for the firing.

That is what anxiety does. It makes you terrified about the future pain and ignores your reality. I understand that I "am hired to be fired," and if I give everything I have to my clients, sometimes, they choose to go in a new direction.

When I hung up, I had this sudden surge of adrenaline. I was sweating profusely, soaking my shirt and pants, which caught the attention of fellow travelers. I was relieved and excited but immediately turned to "Why do I worry like that?" I turned a positive into another worry.

Why? Because I have anxiety.

Start facing what you fear. One step, one detail at a time. When your mind tells you to avoid the stress, lean into it.

How Do You Face It?

You simply start by letting down your defenses. You can withstand the storms of anxiety if you are willing to stand up to those discomforts. You must shift your mindset towards growth and improvement instead of avoidance and fear.

Start facing the minor fears, the tiniest of challenges your mind tells you to avoid. Do not put off calling your coach. Make the call now.

Do not avoid working out. Go as soon as you can.

Do not avoid the negative thoughts and fears in your head. Instead, ask yourself if you can forge forward progress despite the doubts?

Our short-circuit society does not emphasize growth because anxiety wants you to see the pain of the moment. Perfectionism is never about development but instead rooted in the desperate need for validation. Yet, that growth is filled with powerful nuggets of confidence, wisdom, and motivation.

The beauty of this world is growth and development. Start seeing the growth in the minor battles in your mind and trust the future will be better. The future may not be easier, but it surely can be better. I doubt you will have a negative view of the battles you have won that have put you in a better position in the future. Turn anxiety into an invitation to invest in you, not a desire to avoid the pain of the moment.

Is it that simple? Yes.

Face your fears. Face your inner bullies. Focus on growth, even nallest of moments that you worked through.

Teach yourself that you can stand before your fears and endure the storm. Nothing you think can destroy your future if you realize that your self-belief can continually be developed and grown. Therefore, your thinking is never fatal.

12

WHAT YOU FOCUS ON YOU BECOME

Having anxiety will challenge your focus and attention. The details are the victims. You only have so much energy to devote to your daily demands, but when you spend a tremendous amount of energy on factors beyond your control, you have none left for the details of your life.

I travel a ton and love to experience new places. Traveling also spikes my anxiety.

Where do I go when I get to the city?

Where is my hotel?

Where is the rental car counter?

It only worsens when I go out of the country.

It has helped me to focus more on the details, not being stressed by them.

I now take time to organize the details that typically give me stress. I study the airport I am transferring through and learn where the rental car facility is to know where I am going upon arrival.

I can't simply wing it anymore.

It is too stressful to figure things out while trying to manage anxiety.

Having anxiety and being a perfectionist should make you more focused on the details, but the opposite is true. Anxiety robs you of your attention to detail. Well, at least the ones that matter.

When in the throes of a flood of anxiety, your mind becomes flooded with competing demands. The ability to see details gets lost by every approaching threat. Instead of focusing on the details and working through the smaller areas for improvement and progress, you become fixated on the next threat, the next challenge, and the subsequent need to survive.

You must learn to pivot out of that heightened fear and refocus back on the details. Every great competitor and championship program establishes a standard driven by the details. That focus is the hardest thing to do.

It requires a choice – do you focus on what you can control, the smaller elements of your progress, or do you bet on surviving the next threat and then only find the time to focus on what matters? After losses, coaches routinely tell the media, "We need to get back to the basics, doing our jobs and focusing on the fundamentals."

Focusing on the details is a daily battle and not an easy one. I see this battle regularly while working on the PGA TOUR. My players have so many different challenges and demands they must manage day-to-day, week-to-week, that there are times that they get overwhelmed. During regular weeks of the year, they gh equipment testing, fighting swing tendencies, and hysical ailments. The noise intensifies during Major weeks, adding media, travel parties, and corporate responsibilities.

I can often see the clutter in their eyes when they show up to practice. They have their phones in their back pockets, their agents are working around the range, and equipment representatives are hovering while they are trying to practice. Everyone is doing their job, but the challenge intensifies when everyone needs the final decision-maker – the player. And their coaching team is trying to get them ready to compete!

As the competitive rounds approach, the players work hard to quiet that noise but often struggle with where to put their attention. Do they focus on their swing keys? What about course strategy? What worked last week?

When a cluttered mind leads to a missed cut, that is the time to dive in with the player. One of my top-ranked players called very frustrated and disappointed in himself. "Doc, I was so bad this week. My focus was terrible, and I couldn't get locked in," he told me.

I came up with a mental organizational structure that he uses today. I told him that he had allowed the complexity of the circumstance around the event to flood his focus, robbing him of what made him world-class, his mental focus under pressure. It is a common culprit, particularly as a player ascends to the top of the world rankings.

I told him that entering a week on the road, I wanted him to be mentally open to the clutter during the first part of the week. I did not want him to fight it but to refine his preparation plan, declare what he wanted to accomplish each day and communicate it with the team.

By focusing on preparation details, intentional actions would replace competing demands.

As the final day of practice concludes, I wanted him to identify his focus points on three areas of his game – Mental, Physical, and Attitude.

- **Mental** – I wanted him to identify the aspect of his mental game that he would focus on so that no matter how busy his mind would become, regardless of the pressure of the moment, he would always have a focus point.

- **Physical** – As the week of practice concluded, I wanted him to determine what he felt physically that he needed to execute. I anticipate this would stay consistent week-to-week, but the novel feels would hijack his consistent work if he did not clarify it.

- **Attitude** – While this is a part of the mental game, I felt it was essential to bring additional attention to his attitude in competition. When overwhelmed, he typically loses his flexibility and gets judgmental of himself. I needed him to instead declare at moments of low stress what he anticipated when things intensified. I did not want the heightened pressure of anxiety of competition to change his mental and attitude framework.

My player called me after the final day of preparation for the next tournament. He locked into three things and wrote them down in his yardage book. By doing so, he had a reference he could review if he felt he had lost his focus, or his attention had been hijacked.

"Mentally, I will have a clear picture for every shot and describe it to my caddy. The shot will be my focus, and I will make that decision," he told me.

Boom! That sounds simple and obvious. That is the point.

He realized that their on-course process had become very broken, failing to discuss shots in detail and just going through the motions.

"Physically, I went back to the basics of my swing. I am freaking one of the best players in the world, and I have been over-complicating things, trying to be perfect with every shot. Instead, I must accept that my average is better than most in the field, so this will help me do that!"

"Attitude-wise, I want to be accepting of every shot I hit and be a competitor. That is what attracted me to this game. I love getting into the fight and feeling that stress."

By doing that exercise, he returned to the details that drove his success. As anxiety increased leading into an event, he had *the* plan to focus on what mattered the most – his plans for success.

Sometimes, as a coach, you push for a new strategy or a returned focus on the things you feel are important, and it blows up in your face. Other times, it works. This time, it worked.

He went on to win a prestigious tournament in dominating fashion. His focus was so simple, and nothing changed on the outside. The same pressures were there, the same distractions, and he probably had more anxiety following a missed cut. His process changed as he focused on the details that drove the success, not the distractions that anxiety wanted him to focus on.

You must focus on the details in your life. Anxiety wants you to gloss over the details to focus on the drama in the future. Periods of overlooking the little things seem simple initially, but those mistakes add up over time, and you are far away from your goals.

The Details are in the Packaging

The technology giant Apple has consistently demonstrated the value of focusing on the details. It is easy to connect to their highly innovative products and overlook the details that drive their innovation.

The overall design of Apple products is elegant and efficient. There are no duplicative functions and few buttons to operate their products.

The boxes housing the products are sleek, representing a clean, organized design. In Walter Issacson's biography of Apple founder Steve Jobs, he highlighted the importance of the design elements behind Apple products. The product box and delivery process were as crucial as anything else for Jobs.

Why?

The box represents the marketing psychology of anticipation and expectation bias. The elegance and simplicity of the Apple product boxes reflect the precision of the contents inside the box. Your psychological impression starts with your first connection to the product – the box, store, and experience. No detail was insignificant.

The manufacturing industry has taken the direction from Apple and has invested millions of dollars in the details of product boxing. In today's world of online merchants, the psychology driving product boxing has become increasingly important.

Details matter.

Lack of attention to detail destroys progress.

Although details get overlooked in favor of more attention-grabbing distractions, you must value the importance of the details in your psychological life. The slightest deviations from the norm can be anxiety-provoking, yet those details are not appreciated as necessary enough to focus on.

Details Drive Growth

The smallest building blocks provide the foundation for the most prominent skyscrapers. Building a skyscraper may take forever, but much time is devoted to establishing a structurally solid foundation below the surface. Few people ever see the work below the surface.

You must take the time to devote to the details in your:

- Process
- Preparation
- Execution
- Analysis

Do you have a plan for your days?

Do you create a "to-do" list to keep you focused on the most critical needs of the day?

Do you prepare a grocery list or pick up what looks good? If you do the latter, you probably pick up more junk food than you planned. Take that from personal experience.

Success is built upon the decisions of right now. The calm you are searching for is created in the focus of your mind right now.

Do not avoid the little things because there is a greater need. Nothing is more important than doing the little things, gaining positive momentum, and being satisfied with a completed task.

Discipline is the Driver

The second hand on a clock runs at the same rate, whether it is approaching the top of the hour or leaving it. If you feel that particular detail is not worth your time, what specific second is worth more attention?

You only have so much mental energy per day, so you must choose where to devote your focus, but when you avoid your primary responsibilities, the effort takes so much more fixing a problem than doing it right the first time.

No one is born more disciplined than another. Discipline is a choice and prioritization of what you perceive to be necessary. Your upbringing, experiences, and desires determine that importance.

You have to make a choice every day to choose the thoughts, actions, and responses that develop you. It is easy to overlook and ignore things in favor of easier, more enjoyable processes. Success is not always fun. If you avoid your responsibilities, your anxiety will grow.

You either choose to do or choose to avoid. There are few spots in between those two extremes.

The details you ignore are the ones that cause you the most problems down the road. Discipline is a choice 100% of the time. Those with great discipline are not born with a trait that keeps them locked in. They choose to invest their time and energy into the decisions required for their responsibilities.

Anxiety will tell you that something more critical needs your immediate attention. Do not fall for the trap.

Your focus on the details does not stay locked in over time. Something new will distract you, your anxiety will intensify, and a new threat will take you away from what is important. I have yet to meet someone, be associated with a program, and study an organization that remains consistently disciplined to the details. Everyone loses that focus at some point.

The PGA TOUR player I discussed earlier, who won after locking into a new process, had the same issue. Following the victory, distractions intensified. After a few weeks away, he struggled to find that same mental intensity that helped him lock into the details. In a short time, his anxiety intensified, making him increasingly more distracted, frustrated, and judgmental.

He had been doing the same exercises and mental strategies, but his intention needed to be improved. The effort was there, but the intensity driving his focus was different. If you could quantify the decrease in his intention or intensity, you could assume the difference was no more than 5-10%, but it had a dramatic impact. That 5-10% had been reallocated to other distractions, each of which was important on its own but detrimental to his goals.

As his anxiety amplified and frustration grew, he got more judgmental of not "locking in." I explained that the anxiety of poor play, fear of not performing on bigger stages, and frustration of missing valuable opportunities would only contribute to greater struggle. He could not snap his fingers and fix his struggles. It would take focus and directed intention to his process and the details.

Here was the most important thing, however. His returned focus on the details had to be done because it was the right thing to do, not because he anticipated results to follow. His anxiety would not let him play out the process of working the details without that return on the effort.

Our work has focused more on the utility of the details and why they are essential instead of what results will be achieved through working on the details. It has helped, but it is a regular battle in our conversations.

What is the most important thing you must focus on right now? Start there.

13

SUFFER POWERFULLY

The following was a text I received from a professional athlete, cleaned up a little for this book:

> *Doc, I can't do this anymore. The anxiety is crippling me. I do not want to play anymore.*
>
> *I can't do this. I feel so much pressure. My family is putting so much pressure on me. I have become the freaking ATM at this point.*
>
> *Every time I go to the ballpark, my chest hurts, my stomach gets sick, and my head feels like it is in a vice.*
>
> *I want to play the game for me. I don't want to hurt anymore. I hate what this has done to me.*

There is quite a bit to unpack in that text. And yes, this was an actual text.

As an elite professional athlete, he was struggling immensely. His life was no longer about the game but about the layers of the game influencing his life. As a result, his anxiety started to grow, pushing on every boundary and relationship he had in his life.

His only thought was to retreat, escape his environment, and find peace somewhere else. Retirement was on the table, and while he had plenty left to compete with, he focused on escaping from the pain in his life.

My advice is always the same – do not run *from* something, run *to* something.

The pain of anxiety can be brutal. For me, it was nausea and the need to vomit. Others complain of having a heart attack, intense headaches, or feeling like a million bees are flying in their stomach. Anxiety is not in your head but in every part of you.

Anxiety is like playing with fire.

Fire needs heat, fuel, and oxygen to burn. Anxiety needs pressure, fears, and energy to thrive.

That is the problem and why suffering from anxiety cannot be avoided. If you strive for something in your life, you will have anxiety. If you push harder, you risk having anxiety become an obstacle to your growth. That is a fact.

My professional athlete was fixated on his anxiety as the problem. The fact was that he was always "high energy," my favorite descriptor I hear from coaches for an athlete who may appear anxious. That anxiety was his energy source and drove him to push through so much, outcompete more talented players, and persevere through various challenges.

The problem was he changed his focus. Some of it was not his fault, as his family became very dependent upon him for their financial needs. But his external world had compressed down on his internal experiences.

The same fuel he had used to push through had started burning him. For him, his anxiety was the energy that directed his focus.

But when that focus becomes distracted, the suffering of anxic can become painful. He had always had anxiety, but now his outlet had become disrupted.

To help him, we refocused his attention and accepted that his anxiety was part of him and that if he were going to have anxiety, we would use it. Suffering was a reality, but the impact that his anxiety caused in his life ultimately was his choice.

I bet that sounds harsh. It is.

My point is this: he had suffered from anxiety for years. That was the norm, not the exception. The difference was he let that suffering extend to other areas in his life, which brought back so much more pain. He avoided the issue, hoping it would go away – his family's needs from him and the pressure he put on himself.

Instead of taking the anxiety and setting boundaries with his family, he avoided that suffering, only to keep reinvesting where he had some control - in his sport. But over time, that anxiety burned out of control, destroying everything because he lost control. He had to retake control, not get rid of the suffering.

Anxiety is always there. If you have struggles in life, it is not *because* you have anxiety. Instead of seeing suffering from anxiety as the problem, start to use that energy for positive growth.

The fact you suffer doesn't mean crap.

You will always have discomfort or suffering.

Suffering is part of human growth and is the core of the philosophical underpinnings of Buddhism and Stoicism.

controlled, predictable, and stable environments.
e in environments that are chaotic, unstable, and
ing. You cannot equate the comfort of training to
mpetitive success. You must prepare to suffer in
competition and anticipate the challenges.

When you venture towards uncertainty, things will be
uncomfortable. You must prepare to become miserable, doubt
yourself, and face your most terrifying fears. Do not fear the
difficult; anticipate the challenging moments.

There will always be a more demanding tournament or a worse
performance in the future, and those moments should not be
feared but anticipated.

You magnify the suffering when you get confused with
the *WHY* of anxiety. You will reduce suffering if you anticipate
the drama instead of getting caught in the *WHY* loop.

You must uncouple the idea of being comfortable with success.
Being comfortable is not an indicator of success. Being
comfortable in your surroundings, whether in competitive
environments or your internal thought processes, reflects that
you are in less threatening environments. As a psychologist, I see
that as restricting growth.

The edges of your performance and comfort zone are never
comfortable.

Great competitors venture into the unknown and prepare to feel
the disturbing feelings in their gut, the pounding heart rate, and
racing thoughts. The mere existence of those uncomfortable
sensations does not trigger the need to retreat but instead fuels
the desire to push for more. They feel the same intensity as every
competitor, but instead of withdrawing and protecting, they
push forward with intensity and determination.

Going into the unknown is always scary, but it is the only way to grow. I receive phone calls often from frustrated parents about the perceived struggles of their junior athletes.

(Side note: I rarely receive phone calls after victories, which always amuses me and probably contributes to my anxiety.)

The phone calls always suggest that their poor performance is due to a deficiency in their mental game, which the parents often feel predicts a more troublesome future. The parents must understand that getting their players into those often frustrating and challenging competitive environments will build their future successful performances.

If they learn from those moments, that is.

When you suffer, your body and mind experience valuable lessons about how you perform, think, and persist in depths of uncertainty and struggle. You must develop an analytical approach to review how you felt, what you thought, and where you doubted your ability to progress.

Those lessons can be critical because you will get into those circumstances again, but if you fail repeatedly, you must learn to see the lessons within the misery.

Frustration and doubt are fueled by learning. Without those moments of frustration and doubt, comfort sets in, and you move away from the edges of comfort. Be prepared to suffer because that is where the most significant learning will emerge.

Suffering through the learning blocks does not indicate stagnation—quite the opposite. Your performance struggle and your mind's anxieties teach you what to trust through your progress. Your power is never revealed in the calm. When suffering can open to learning possibilities, you emerge from the darkness of doubt into realizing opportunities.

When you open yourself up to the potential of suffering, you learn that you can endure anything, which is the true definition of confidence.

Social Comparisons

Several years ago, one of my professional athletes took me to a personal development seminar for my birthday. I had always wanted to see the speakers on the agenda that day, notably Tony Robbins and Gary Vaynerchuk. I always loved their styles and found their respective confidence on stage inspiring.

One of the lesser-known speakers on the agenda that day caught my attention, however, but not in a good way. When this speaker took the stage, she began speaking about the power of "not caring what your haters think about you." Her whole presentation was about becoming so obsessed with your excellence that the opinions of others will no longer matter.

The crowd was fired up! They were yelling and screaming, holding onto every word.

My professional athlete colleague looked at me during the presentation and asked, "How can I not care what people think?"

"You can't; it is part of you being a human. What she is telling everyone is impossible unless you are a sociopath," I told him.

The opinions of others matter. It is part of the evolutionary cycle of human beings because social status is critical for general advancement. If you do not care what the people around you think, you are not striving to improve your status.

It is that simple.

As humans, we are invested in the opinions of others. They do matter!

This simple fact is why social media is so powerful in today's culture. A "like" or repost of a status update serves as validation of approval, even from strangers.

I want you to care about what others think, but I want you to understand what you can control in others' opinions.

You have no idea what someone values as important, what battles they are personally facing, or even what you do that creates stress in their self-image. You must realize that your projections onto others often reflect your insecurities, not highlight your strengths.

Use the Suffering for Good

I am who I am because of my anxiety. I have learned that I have periods when the anxiety hurts and times when it seems inconsequential.

I worry.

I stress.

I sometimes avoid what needs to be said or done.

I see the worst in the future.

I run every negative outcome possible from the smallest pieces of evidence.

I write the ending before the beginning ever happe

But anxiety does not have to go away for me to succeed.

I can thrive with anxiety.

I can do more with anxiety than without it.

I can find freedom in my life with or without anxiety.

What is the worst that can happen? I make a mistake, get fired, or miss a shot? I can work through it.

I can own what I feel without judging it.

I can suffer *with* anxiety. I can feel intensely *with* anxiety.

I can be powerful with or without anxiety.

I have learned that anxiety is a part of me, good and bad. Sometimes, I feel more anxiety; other times, I use that anxiety to overcome something difficult.

Like everything in my life, if I am going to have something, do something, or manage with something, I am doing it powerfully.

I am going to suffer powerfully because my power comes from my anxiety. There is no freedom unless I accept who I am and what makes me who I am. I will suffer powerfully because I am not going to run from it.

Start to suffer powerfully because I will never give up my power.

14

BUILD A PROCESS FOR YOUR LIFE

Every year, sports franchises and college athletic departments spend significant financial resources to change their leadership, including head coaches, athletic directors, and general managers. Those drastic changes leverage the desire for the improved organizational performance through new coaching philosophies, better accountability, or improved cultures. Fans get excited, leading to increased expectations for the team's success, only to see the same frustrating cycle repeat season after season.

I talked with an elite sports agent who represents coaches about why coaches continue to fail and how this coaching-change cycle keeps spinning. He said something very insightful about the drivers of the continuous change – a lack of process.

He said many programs and professional franchises lack clear leadership and direction, basing personnel and coaching decisions on emotion. When the teams start losing, they lack the direction to lead a team through the struggles. The only obvious decision when the organization is lost is to change leadership and hope for someone to inspire confidence and leadership.

Unfortunately, finding coaches who have a distinct process and can execute it is daunting. The good ones are employed and having success. They only want to leave a program that is having success to take a risk with a troubled organization if the price is right!

When discussing great programs, you hear the terms "culture, process, and system" all the time. But what was the sports agent referring to?

The sports agent laid it out for me. He said every coach has their system for in-game strategy, or at least they can describe it to their administration or booster groups. They all have a system in place for recruiting talent. They may also have one for building a winning culture throughout the organization.

While they may have a process or system, do they have one that wins, sustains success, and builds an unbeatable culture?

He said that an actual process goes deep into the details, from player development per position to the personality styles of assistant coaches to what time practice starts and the rationale behind it. He said detractors label rival coaches with comprehensive processes as micromanagers, but the best have a plan for everything.

As a result, when the team struggles, the coach is not lost, emotionally reacting to difficulties, just hoping to find success. Instead, they have the plan to execute, and likely, a plan tested over years of experience.

Regardless of their sport, the best coaches in the world build success through their philosophy, vision, and the process built to achieve those desires. The most successful educate their programs on the process and build buy-in, helping players and their assistant coaches funnel their energy into executing the process, not chasing quick fixes.

Finding those great coaches can be difficult, but you can always find the successful ones by finding evidence of lasting success.

Those programs win year after year, achieving success through various circumstances and with different contributors. The system driving the process is built more extensively than having success in one moment, one superstar player, or good luck.

Most importantly, those with great processes do not overreact to challenging situations, a bad loss, or an untimely injury to a star player. Those coaches invest their anxiety, stress, and energy into their daily decisions and actions instead of making emotional decisions that do not last.

Columnist Paul Myerberg of *USA Today* examined the critical traits of hiring college football coaches in a December 6, 2022, article entitled <u>What makes successful college football coaching hire? A look at Power Five hires finds key traits</u>. According to his research, 43 hires occurred in Power Five schools (e.g., schools from the five largest conferences in college football) from 2018-21, and only 44.2% were considered successful hires. Seven schools had to hire more than one head coach during that time! Not only is that tremendous turnover, but it also highlights the difficulty of building a successful program.

Myerberg concluded the most successful hires had several prior years of experience coaching in the Power Five conferences (the most competitive schools), were older, had an offensive focus, and were connected to the school somehow. Those are all great conclusions, but a deeper dive is necessary.

Those with experience in the Power Five conferences hired by another program must have demonstrated success to be viable candidates. Unsuccessful coaches are not marketable. Older coaches get older by staying in the profession, using their wisdom year after year to stay successful in the game.

Successful offensive coaches who elevate to head coaches do so because of their play-calling systems that exploit the weaknesses of their opponents by matching them up against their team's strengths. A coach cannot fake an offensive strategy.

Each trait reflects a definitive process, refined over time, and tested against the most challenging opponents. Over time, those processes that adapt and grow get better, and those that do not or get caught up reacting to every struggle get passed over.

As the challenge increases, the process becomes more critical.

What Does a Process Have to Do with Anxiety?

Anxiety builds urgency to act, but that is not always good. The more anxious you feel, the more you want to get out of the discomfort and find peace of mind. As the discomfort rises, your ability to make informed decisions decreases. Without a process driving your decisions and actions, you are nothing more than making short-term reactions and searching for relief.

The urgency to get better drives energy and effort, but what if that effort is misdirected?

Imagine you showed up at my office, and I told you and your team that there was $10 million buried in the land behind my house. I bet you would have a strong commitment to finding it.

Would you start digging immediately? Where? How deep?

Without those questions answered you would wear yourself out.

Would you start by surveying the land? You could, but the land's topography may not tell you about the location of the money.

How would you get started?

Too often, you get started without a direction, process, or plan. Instead, you forge forward with all the urgency and energy possible without focusing on a strategy to succeed. Sometimes, you succeed, but more times than not, you experience significant frustration and quit long before finding success.

I bet you think, "If there were $10 million, I would never quit!" Yes, you would. Your lack of efficiency would eventually lead to you accepting failure. It is hard to stay motivated when all you experience is failure.

The best competitors in the world rely on systematic processes to drive their success. I have played for the best, coached for the best, and currently work with the best to ever do it – they all have a process that drives their performance success. It does not matter if they have anxiety, fear, doubts, or world-class confidence.

The best trust their process no matter what is happening around them.

The best develop a series of planned actions and perspectives that anchor them when things get complicated.

Anxiety finds the cracks in your processes.

If Chick-fil-A planned to open a new restaurant in your neighborhood, there would be a series of well-designed and strongly communicated systems in place. Everything would be systematically laid out to increase the odds of success against any unforeseen challenges.

Onboarding new employees follows a distinct process, so they begin to execute on the standards consistent with Chick-fil-A. They practice refining their systems so that when customers visit the store, they are ready for the influx of business.

There is a reason Chick-fil-A can handle success better than any other fast food restaurant in the market.

Misery thrives in chaos. Chaos provides the fertile ground for more anxiety to develop.

If you lack a process in your life, you are flying without instructions. You are trying to be an expert but need more processes to succeed.

Anxiety wants you to see everything that is wrong around you, and it thrives when you struggle to be productive.

I have spent years around the two greatest coaches ever in their sports. Both had a system or process driving their success. It was not a mistake that Skip Bertman and Nick Saban dominated their athletics landscape. Both could have run Fortune 100 companies simply because they excelled at finding ways to implement processes into chaotic organizations.

Tom Brady did not become the greatest quarterback in the NFL because of his talent level alone. Then again, success is not a talent contest. Brady became the best because he had an internal drive that built a process for continued success. His method – TB12 – was created to become the best.

Anxiety wants to find the gaps in your systems and works to knock you down or erode the ground from underneath you. Anxiety will destroy you if you do not focus on building an unbreakable system. Anxiety is uncomfortable, but I don't want it to become destructive.

There are four steps to creating a potent personal system – a dream, a philosophy, a game plan, and a measuring stick.

A Desire

What do you want to achieve? If you want to be out of discomfort from anxiety, that is not a purpose. I want you to establish a goal to achieve something you want *despite* your level of anxiety. It does not matter what you are feeling.

If you can lock into your vision, you can work towards achieving it.

Anxiety will tell you that you cannot achieve your goals, your circumstances are too challenging, and you are not tough enough to endure the struggle. Who can determine if your desires are worthy of your efforts?

I sat with one player and had this exact conversation. He was a very talented player but needed development. He was not ready to compete, and his developmental time frame was longer than most. Some coaches may call him a project, but his timeline was longer than others.

He had struggled early in practice, and his coach recommended he see me. I asked him directly, "Why did you come here when the odds are so low for you to succeed? You could have gone elsewhere in the country to be a star, but you are buried on the depth chart here.

The coaches will out-recruit you every single year."

His response was fantastic – "Doc, I didn't come here because it would be easy. My goals are difficult, and I deserve the toughest place to play to make me the best version of myself. When I leave here, the fans and coaches will consider me 'one of the best to do it.'"

I was struck by his confidence, even bordering on his arrogance. He desired to be one of the best, so he had to match it with effort. That was my challenge.

He did – and he is one of the best to do it in college. Statistics do not lie, and championships last forever.

You cannot have a Plan B.

Do you want a surgeon who tried medical school or one who dreamt about performing life-saving surgeries their whole life?

Anxiety seduces you into believing you must hedge your bets and find a soft-landing place.

Go all in!

If you fall short of your dreams, you will adjust.

Plan B's do nothing more than give you an easy out.

A dear friend spent 12 years in the US Navy as a SEAL. One of his assignments was to prepare candidates for BUDS – the brutal, 6-month training program that grinds through SEAL candidates, resulting in a tremendous drop-out rate.

He bragged that his graduates had the highest completion rates of BUDS on record.

Why?

He made every candidate write a letter describing why they wanted to be a Navy SEAL. He found that guys with no alternatives in the Navy were willing to push through the significant challenges to succeed.

If they were in training because of vanity, to become a SEAL because it was cool to do, or even if they just wanted to see if they could do it, they would find their breaking point individually.

They could find a way if they had nothing else to do – SEAL or nothing.

No Plan Bs. Set a vision of what you want. What are you afraid of?

You may not make it.

Settling for mediocrity and a life of regret does not inspire you to become the best version of yourself.

1. A Philosophy

Successful organizations, from sports teams to businesses, work around a collective organizational culture that reflects the team's desires, each contributor's role, and the organization's overarching mission. Ultimately, this culture represents the philosophy of the leadership of the organization.

Individuals often fail to identify or stand behind a definitive philosophy in life. Instead, life starts living you, and the goal becomes survival. Day by day is nothing but surviving until the next break.

You must identify how you want to live your life, and I am talking about your guiding principles that contribute to the nature of your life.

While many religions and spiritual paths involve developing personal philosophies, I want you to expand on those foundational elements and build yours out even more.

Consider the following questions as a starting point:

· What does struggle mean to you? In your life? In your competitive arena?

· What is the importance of people in your life? What role do you see for those inside your inner circle versus those on the periphery?

· How do you balance stress, life demands, expectations, and opinions of others?

· What are your coping mechanisms? When life gets difficult, where do you find your strength?

Developing a powerful philosophy requires more reflection than reaction. You have to work to be true to your authentic self. Authenticity can be one of the hardest things to do because it requires total vulnerability and honesty.

I know what I want in life, but I struggled to establish my philosophy in my professional life. Professionally, I knew I thought differently than my colleagues, and that created significant self-doubt.

When I started graduate school, I lacked experience in traditional psychology settings common among undergraduates, such as research laboratories or treatment centers. Because I changed my undergraduate major very late in my undergraduate career, I always felt behind my colleagues. Not only did I not have their experiences, but I also had a different perspective on psychology. With such little experience in psychology settings, I was much more skeptical of the "standards" of commonly accepted psychological frameworks.

Don't get me wrong – I did not reject the traditional perspectives in psychology because I wanted to be a disrupter. Not at all.

What was normal in applying psychology did not seem normal to me.

When I started providing professional sport and performance psychology services, I tried to emulate those succeeding in the field as consultants. I would watch videos of other performance coaches and study how they spoke, captivated the audience, and explored the themes of their talks. I wasn't trying to copy them, but I needed to explore their styles and content.

All it did was frustrate me.

No one else was me. No one is me.

I had to accept that I formed my performance philosophy through my competitive experiences, educational foundation as a clinical psychologist, and early professional encounters. My philosophy reflected my experiences more than a theoretical framework crafted in a laboratory.

You have a way you want to "do" life – both in competition and everyday living. You must gain insight into your perspective and build your philosophy. Not everyone has to approve of it, and so long as it does not take advantage of other people, you are better off living your philosophy than fitting into someone else's.

2. A Game Plan

It is easier to be consistent if you have a process guiding your actions. Offensive coordinators in football often script the first 20 plays of a football game and call plays in relative order. The rationale is that early in a football game, the offensive coordinator wants to get the offense working in a rhythm and does not want to get distracted from the events happening in the game. They want to work in different foundational plays to build confidence and achieve positive momentum.

The same mindset can work for you and help you establish a process that will defeat the attacks launched by anxiety.

What are the key elements you want to accomplish every day?

What are your strengths?

What are your anchors when the day gets chaotic or your anxiety spikes?

When do you want to exercise – morning, lunch, or after a long day?

When do you want to meditate – morning, lunch, or after a long day?

All those factors are critical to building a game plan to drive your process.

3. A Measuring Stick

"Doc, I just want to be happy. That is all I want," my client told me. I understood what he meant, but I had no idea what he wanted to feel.

I do not know how to measure happiness. The same could be said for many emotions.

That is the problem when you define your outcomes based on feelings. Measuring an outcome based on a feeling is very difficult to do proactively.

Sometimes, the most incredible insights come in the strangest places. For me, one powerful perspective came from a favorite sitcom of mine, *The Office*. Ed Helm's character, Andy Bernard, said, "I wish there was a way to know you are in the good ole days before you have actually left them."

Brilliant.

Powerful.

Truth.

I want you to have a measuring stick for your process so that you can know your progress. Few people know how to measure progress, as far too many jump from challenge to challenge, fail to appreciate moments of growth and happiness, and, as a result, struggle to survive the grind of life.

The best measuring stick happens by journaling progress. Start recording things where you have positive outcomes and write down learnings from the areas you are struggling with. Use your daily experiences as your measuring stick, and then you will start to identify the appropriate incremental steps driving your progress.

Your process expresses your desires, but you must have more depth than simply a desire. You must have a plan to drive your effort and measure it.

Just Trust the Process

I have been around two coaches (Skip Bertman and Nick Saban) who relied heavily on their processes or systems to drive their success. Coach Bertman taught "The System" to his players throughout his tenure and would have Friday night meetings to review individual elements that he felt were important to success. For instance, he would review how to line up for the pregame Pledge of Allegiance, back up an overthrow, or even the itinerary for the national title game in June in an October meeting. Every element was necessary for success, so Bertman took the time and prioritized it.

Coach Nick Saban emphasizes "The Process," his approach to focus the mind on the little details that influence success instead of losing your focus on the score of a game. Saban's approach emphasizes "how you do something" in practice so you can trust your overlearned technique, decisions, and grit in a game.

When players from their programs utter "trust the process" or "trust the system," it is not simply words. Both of their alums live their approaches off the field as well, and when I get with my baseball teammates or meet with former players I coached at the University of Alabama, those impressions still guide them. You can see the evidence in the words they speak, the actions they take, and the impact they make on others.

Have you ever met a former member of the military? You know it when you speak with them and can see the clues in every element of their life. The military process becomes part of their DNA. It is not just saying to "trust the process." You must live it every single moment of your life.

You built your process to endure the good and bad of life, so you must trust every aspect of it.

You must live every part of the process. You must resist the urges for short-term relief and focus on continued determination and effort. If you are seeking relief from your anxiety, there is no definitive process. You can get relief, but the relief you experience will not last. The pain will build in the vacuum left behind and come back stronger.

The pain of following a process does not create the vacuum that short-term relief creates. When you follow a process, you build confidence and success through smaller successes, strengthening your resolve to face the next challenge. A process stacks successes on top of each other and provides a foundation when you feel the most vulnerable.

In your battles with anxiety, resist the urge to chase short-term fixes and invest that energy in building a process for your daily life.

I have a process for quieting a busy mind – I write down my thoughts.

I learned a meditation trick years ago to combat the anxiety I feel when I am trying to fall asleep, and it works wonders.

I have a process for attacking busy days – I lay out a plan.

I have a process for writing books – I write sentences and thoughts at coffee shops until my voice wakes up in the manuscript.

I have a process for working on the PGA Tour – every player has a distinct plan to match their psychological fingerprint.

I have processes on top of processes, but every individual process helps me manage my anxiety and center my focus.

I have found that if I face my anxiety with a structured plan of attack, I build processes that help me the next time I am struggling. By devoting my energy to the specific process, I funnel the physical and mental energy into actionable steps designed to drive results. As a result, those steps do not need me to feel good, calm, or even confident because I know those processes work regardless of how I feel.

15

BUILD YOUR SUPPORT

Fans see the on-field successes of professional athletes and celebrate their talents, skills, and tenacity after every great victory. Still, they rarely get access to their off-the-field worlds. The greatest competitors in the world did not get there by themselves. The athlete is responsible for their success, but there have been many contributors helping them build the successful structure to make it happen.

I am a member of several large support teams for my professional athletes. It is not uncommon for professional athletes to employ multiple experts to help them be ready to compete in the most significant moments.

The teams often include nutritionists, massage therapists, physiologists, strength and conditioning performance coaches, technical and sport-specific mechanics specialists, agents, financial coaches, psychologists or mental conditioning coaches, and physical therapists. An athlete earning $10 million annually in the arena can easily spend over a million per year on their teams.

Remember that the difference between being an All-Star, a Hall-of-Famer, a role player, or even a flash-in-the-plan can be a series of tiny incremental differences. If their bodies are a touch slower than their competition, that can be the difference between making the big play or being ridiculed on every sports talk station in the country.

Living and performing with anxiety can be isolating. No one truly knows the depth of your fears, understands the pain of the irrational thoughts, and has to live in your skin when amped beyond the norm while trying to look normal. Sure, you can try to "fake it until you make it," but that is just a constant reminder that you are a fraud.

Or so you fear.

Do you think those around you would judge you differently because you have anxiety? How do you know they do not suffer from the same pain?

Are you sure they do not struggle with more than you? You are never alone. Avoid the temptation to retreat in your fears and isolate yourself from those in your life.

The Watchdog

In the final minutes of Super Bowl XLIX, The New England Patriots struggled to stop a game-winning drive from the Seattle Seahawks. As the Seahawks approached the line of scrimmage in the game's final seconds, they only needed to score a touchdown, and the game would essentially be over. By running the ball down the field and utilizing high-percentage passes, the Seahawks quarterback, Russell Wilson, was surgically beating the Patriots defense.

Wilson and his coach, Pete Carroll, did not want to score too soon because it would leave too much time for the Patriots to answer the touchdown. All they would need would be a field goal, and with future Hall of Famer Tom Brady leading the

Patriots, it seemed too likely that any time left on the clock would be advantageous for Brady and the Patriots.

In those final seconds, the Seahawks were within a yard of scoring a touchdown when Malcolm Butler etched his name in Super Bowl history with a dramatic interception, ending the game and winning the Super Bowl for the Patriots. As a result, Butler became a hero in the football communities, and his play always gets shown celebrating the unlikely victory.

But there is more to the story than a simple interception, the contract and bonuses that Butler earned, and the "hero" play that highlighted that the Seahawks should have run the ball with their bruising, powerful running back – Marshawn Lynch.

In the two weeks leading up to the Super Bowl, coaching staffs prepare for every possible scenario they may encounter during the game. The head coach of the Patriots, Bill Belichick, is often regarded as one of the most prepared coaches in the game.

As the game clock wound down in that fateful Super Bowl, his assistant coaches kept asking Belichick if he wanted to take a time out. In theory, taking a time-out would stop the clock and give the Patriots more time to answer the expected touchdown of the Seahawks. Belichick just listened to his assistant coaches and watched the game play out.

In the most significant moment of the year, Belichick just watched the game play out.

It was not until an NFL Films special, "Do Your Job," aired that it became apparent why Belichick knew what to do.

Ernie Adams was one of Belichick's longest-tenured and trusted research professionals with the Patriots, tasked to identify any and every angle to help the Patriots win. In the preparation leading up to the Super Bowl, Adams had identified the potential for a specific play the Seahawks may run near the goal line. Because they had a powerful running back in Lynch, Adams believed a pick-play would free a receiver on the goal line and make it an easy pass completion, while the defense would sell out for a run.

Adams prepared the team for the play, and Belichick routinely ran the play in preparation when down on the goal line. There was no question that the Seahawks would target Butler, but Butler was not even supposed to be in that position at that part of the game.

Butler was not a superstar at this point. He was an obscure cornerback from Division II University of West Alabama, not quite the powerhouse as the team an hour to their east – The University of Alabama.

Butler subbed into the game in the 4th quarter when his teammate and rookie Kyle Arrington kept getting beat on pass plays, and Belichick felt that Butler would be a better defender for those plays.

Even though Butler had practiced the play, he struggled with the execution. This play was challenging for even the most veteran of defensive backs because the two wide receivers would cross coming off the line of scrimmage, creating a roadblock, freeing up the one wide receiver to the sideline, and opening a passing lane without much defense. In practice, Butler kept getting stuck in the roadblock and struggled to stop the play.

In the most significant moment of the Super Bowl, Belichick just watched and trusted his players. With the final seconds clicking off the clock, it seemed inevitable that the Seahawks would run Lynch.

Belichick hoped they would try to run the passing play, betting on a pick play over the power of the running game. Butler was not even on the field as the Seahawks broke their huddle.

Belichick subbed out a linebacker, Akeem Ayers, with Butler, taking out the physical muscle of a linebacker for the reaction of a defensive back.

As the Seahawks broke the huddle, they lined up with three wide receivers, an adjustment the heavily prepared assistant coaches of the Patriots had noticed when they sent in Butler. Just before the snap, Patriots safety Brandon Browner adjusted Butler to get him in position to jump the route, the only way to defend the pick play. At the snap, Butler zeroed in on the space where the pick would happen and jumped the route, intercepting the pass intended for Seahawks wide receiver Ricardo Lockette.

Butler's interception secured the Super Bowl for the Patriots and made Butler a hero.

The true heroes stood in the shadows that day – Ernie Adams, Browner, and the scout team who ran the play repeatedly.

Surely, Butler could have made the play without all the help, but he relied on his team to help him succeed.

Who Stands in Your Shadows

Anxiety can make you feel alone, exposed, vulnerable, and shaking for all the world to judge. Those thoughts running in your head can be very isolating, especially if you worry that you are the only one with those negative thoughts.

Who can help you if your thoughts are so extreme?

The support teams my professional athletes build are a mosaic of personalities. The support teams I am on have a wide range of personalities, as some team members are brutally honest, and others do their job, do it quite well and avoid public attention. What matters is that every team member serves the athlete's needs.

The most successful athletes understand those different dynamics and build experts who bring something unique. Most of us rely on each other, making the teams successful. If one of my players is struggling, I quickly call and ask another team member for their input, looking for any angle and studying anything I can to help my player. I do not want my players to suffer alone, and when millions of dollars are on the line, I want them to stand confidently in front of any challenge.

That is the same as working in my college setting or even with my private clientele. Over the past ten years, larger college athletic departments have built comprehensive teams to support student-athletes. With those increasing standards and unrealistic expectations athletes face today, they need people to trust and stand on the shoulders of those serving them.

While you may not have a million dollars to build your team, you do not need it to enhance your production. Anxiety will tell you that you don't need more people because they will not understand, but that is the lie of anxiety. You must build a team of those who challenge, support, and enhance you. I see comprehensive teams built around athletes as early as high school, and it is fantastic. As I said earlier, I am witnessing college football players arriving on campus on their first day of college with training teams supporting their development from their hometown. I love that.

To build support around you, you must know what you want out of the relationship before simply hiring or recruiting people around you. You do not need to pay anyone if friends, coaches, or colleagues serve those roles. You must have a plan before asking others for their opinions, ideas, or suggestions.

Early in my career, I would ask anyone for business advice, and I realized that I was asking too many "experts" who did not have a clue about my business and found myself chasing every suggestion they made. It did not matter that they did not understand the nature of psychological boundaries or building healthy relationships. Honestly, had I trusted what I knew, I would have been more successful and saved considerable money. So please be careful about who you surround yourself with.

My father was a retired Lieutenant Colonel in the US Air Force and was a navigator for c-130 aircraft. His role was to serve those on the plane or get supplies to those who needed them on the ground. He used to tell me, "The best teammates, the best coaches, and leaders stand in the shadows, setting up others for success. When you are part of a team, never make it about you. Let someone else have the spotlight."

That advice has stuck with me my entire professional life. I have had clients hire me who shared that the terms of their relationship with other coaches were to promote them on social media or in media interviews. I ask that all my clients refrain from mentioning me at all. I want them to have the spotlight, and the fact that I helped them reflects on them, not me. They listened and applied the material in the most demanding competitive moments.

Anxiety can make you desperate for anyone who promises relief and solutions to your struggles. Since all you want is for the game to be easier, anxiety makes you vulnerable to false promises. The promise can always be greater than the delivery in those situations. Be careful.

In *The MindSide Manifesto*, my first book, I planned to build a circle of trusted advisors around you. I talk about it in nearly every book I write and podcast. It is important; I will lay it out again in this book. If you have heard it before, do not gloss over it.

You may read something that adds to what you already know.

You need five people on your team, each serving a different role. You can have more than one person in each group, but you do not see one performing more than one role. They may have characteristics of different roles but see them in the primary role they provide.

1. Colleague

A colleague is someone who is currently or has been in the same role as you and understands the unique challenges of your position. For instance, I have one professional golfer who leans heavily on a friend who played the tour twenty years prior, spending weekends at his house occasionally. The insight that a former tour professional can provide him is significant, as it helps my player translate instructional cues, filter out doubts, and, in a way, normalize his struggles. Find someone who has been in your shoes and will not judge your "strange" questions and feelings.

2. Competitor

Competition makes everyone better. You need to identify the competition, even if your competitors realize their role in your development. Identify someone who pushes you, makes you get out of your comfort zone, and makes you challenge yourself.

I have a particular influencer in the field that I love to study. Studying their writings, posts, and work products shows tremendous respect because they conduct their business with the highest integrity. They do not glorify who their clients are to market their services. Instead, they produce content that makes a difference. Their content is life-changing, and I have no idea who they work with reading the valuable insights. I love that! Every day, their work motivates me to do better. I am not jealous of their success; their success motivates me to improve daily.

3. Confidence Builder

The road to success can be long and very isolating. Sometimes, your confidence tank rests on empty, and you need someone in your circle who replenishes your confidence.

This person is not a rah-rah person but someone who can point out your progress when you feel lost, exhausted, and hopeless. Confidence builders can also share the truth, but in doing so, they often provide the light in your greatest darkness.

In team sports, there is often an assistant coach on the coaching staff to whom the players gravitate because they are the trusted buffer. Do not go to the well too often but know where to go when you need that person.

4. Challenger

The final two individuals are not warm and fuzzy but critical for growth. The Challenger provides direct, honest, and developmental feedback - never accepting your good is good enough. A Challenger sees the whole picture and knows what your potential could be, never taking success as a time to rest.

Challengers often get players a bit nervous, but they also know how to provide a compliment or spark confidence when you least expect it.

5. Critiquer

Finally, the Critiquer embodies many of the characteristics of a Challenger but does not care if you like them. Honesty is their currency, and being blunt is part of their delivery.

Critiquers often are the seasoned coaches who have seen it all and deliver the straight facts, regardless of how you feel. They are essential, however, because they will be entirely truthful to you even if you do not want them.

If you have ever sent a book to an editor, you know what this feels like. Your paper comes back looking like it had been at a crime scene! You cannot avoid Critiquers; their insight is often the advice you cherish the most years later.

You do not need to deal with your anxiety alone. When you suffer from negative thoughts or crushing insecurities, you need someone who understands your suffering. Anxiety is often perceived as the villain, but your judgment of your feelings is the real criminal. Having people in your corner, working from the shadows to promote your growth and development, will only push you further.

In Super Bowl XLIV, Butler stood on the platform with Brady and celebrated the victory. Ernie Adams, the trusted advisor, watched from a distance, proud that his team made the plays when they had to. He was not in the organization to self-promote; instead, he was there to promote those on the field, and Adams was fine with that.

Adams retired from the New England Patriots in 2021. After nearly twenty years with the Patriots and a fifty-year friendship with Belichick, Adams quietly stepped away, just how he wanted to – to serve those well in his tenure and drift back into the shadows.

16

BE PATIENT

There is something about anxiety that creates impatience and urgency about the future. You cannot correct the past, and you cannot predict the future. When you look at your future, the only thing you know is that it is unknown. That fact creates anxiety.

The urgency of the mind to escape struggle or the desire to build success intensifies over time. In the age of efficiency and technological innovations, skills and athletic abilities have improved much faster. Does one athlete who improves on a faster training plan mean they are better?

Of course not. However, the athlete on the slower plan will have more significant uncertainty about their future, mainly because there is no guarantee that they will reach the levels of success as the faster athlete.

There are no guarantees the faster athlete will progress beyond where they are now, stay at that level of success, or even get derailed by struggles in the future. If you asked both athletes who were more confident in their futures, I would bet the faster athlete would be. Why? The recent successes boost confidence for the future. The slower athlete would not feel that same confidence and have more doubts about their future.

But nothing has changed other than their predictions of the future. The longer it takes, the harder it gets. The harder it gets, the more anxiety builds, and the more impatience grows.

What time frame is appropriate to have success?

Is there a chart that identifies when learning should suddenly become a success?

Who defines if someone is ready to compete, capable of advancement, or even ready to overcome?

There is a force fighting against you, and it is not anxiety – it is impatience.

The self-development industry is ripe with fake promises of rapid improvements. You won't lose fifty pounds in a month (at least healthy), you won't throw 100 MPH due to a three-week throwing program, and you will not stop suffering simply by reading this book. Refrain from falling for the promise of fast at the expense of growth.

Success takes time, despite what your anxiety is telling you. The definition of success changed over time. Moving up through the ranks is not as attractive as overnight success. Someone is not more successful because they reached the top faster than another athlete, played earlier, or struggled less. Unless a defined timeline is required to complete the task, time is irrelevant for development.

Coaches feel the time crunch, too. They fear losing players to the transfer portal if they share that the player's developmental plan requires more than a season. Players quickly transfer to another school when the new coach promises immediate playing time, despite no track record of player development.

I sat down with a very talented player one summer afternoon. His parents were with him because they were concerned with his mental state and felt he was struggling to find a role on the team. It was the middle of the summer and still three months from the first game, but the player was upset that he was not being talked about in the media, not selected to lead training groups, and was the target of his coach in training sessions.

"Every day, I am the focus of his attention. It is getting old," the player told me.

"Why is Coach so hard on you right now? What is he saying that is upsetting to you?" I asked him.

It is important to note that this player had all the physical tools to play in the National Football League (NFL). He was a five-star player who looked the part. He was smart, a great student, and a quality human from a fantastic family.

He was heavily recruited and a great addition to our team. The problem was that he needed help with feedback. He wanted to play immediately, as he believed that was the promise of the recruitment.

When talking to his position coach, that was never the promise. During the recruitment, the coaching staff created a developmental plan for him for his family to see their vision. The entire family bought in.

Somewhere between the recruitment and arriving on campus, he lost that vision.

The assessment was that he was NFL-ready, despite never playing a down in college football. He had freaky physical skills but did not have the insight or awareness to separate himself from more mentally developed student-athletes. Those on the depth chart ahead of him saw the game a half-second faster than him. While those athletes had been through the same trials and struggles as he was, they learned how to adapt and gain the edge to succeed.

This player wanted success without the investment. He perceived the direct coaching feedback as slights of his ability rather than investments into developing his tools. Let me stress that he was an amazing young man. He did not carry a defiant attitude at all, but instead, he was riddled with anxiety about why he was being coached.

"Coaching" implied that he was not performing well enough for the coach's approval. Instead of seeing coaching as a developmental investment into his future, he perceived the attention as rejecting his tools. For today's players, the idea that development takes time often implies that they are not inherently good enough to compete.

In the recent past, developmental progress was a sign of success, a journey highlighted by coaches, and a badge of honor among players. Now, it gets perceived as fixing deficiencies. It is a shame to see it that way, but society is so focused on overnight successes that the attention never finds those who build success. Each of us must be allowed to improve over time.

The player I am referencing chose to stay in school and plays in the NFL. The conversations in that room with his parents remain locked in secrecy, but it took tremendous insight to see the long-term plan was a better investment than any short-term promise.

The Patience of Job

When I was a child, I was not the most patient kid. As an only child, I could get what I usually wanted without much resistance. If you are an only child, you know that game.

One day, my mom brought me a book from the Catholic diocese and asked me to read it. As a young Catholic child, I always enjoyed reading books about the Saints, and the stories of those who endured, overcame, and established the example of living a fulfilled life. I would often read the stories of the Saints more than sports stories. I was a bit weird.

This book was about Job, a man whose writings appear in the Old Testament as the Book of Job. Job was a wealthy man who seemingly had everything he wanted until, as the story tells, God took away all of Job's successes to test his loyalty. Suddenly, Job found himself destitute, challenged to find faith without material blessings.

Despite nearly every possible challenge, Job always retained his faith, believing in gaining wisdom rather than accumulating success. His endurance without immediate relief demonstrates a conflict in today's world, and Job's perspective is critical to delaying the relief and gratification needed now.

I hear so often that success drives confidence, faith, and belief. Yet, the enduring vision loses power when those individual successes take longer than desired. Short-term successes hijack your attention, seducing you to immediate relief from the pain at the expense of the development of wisdom.

Job did not have it easy, and was not devoid of doubt or questioning, but found his way to endure through the trials. His patience is now seen as an example of someone who never gave up and believed in the vision for a future over time, not immediate gratification. Short-term gratification's allure will destroy your wisdom's development, and wisdom is the only proper antidote to anxiety.

Anxiety makes you impatient, a byproduct of the heightened energy anxiety produces. If patience were part of anxiety, you would feel so much worse, reaching a point of absolute misery.

You are not a patient person. Competitors, business leaders, and even somewhat motivated achievers cannot be patient and succeed simultaneously.

When experiencing the full blossom of anxiety, the urgency to escape the immediate discomfort is the most potent motivation in your mind.

Any growth or progression you have experienced requires time, experience, and patience. Things do not come easy, and they will not be systematic.

Patience is about separating yourself from the outcomes you want. Yes, you want to succeed and achieve success, but when you attach your emotional value to your outcomes, you will become increasingly impatient with each struggle. You will become more judgmental and overvalue negative thoughts and doubts than progress.

I have never been patient and do not know how to "trust the process," but I try my best. I also accept that the destination will not alleviate my negative thoughts, doubts, or insecurities.

I will also change the final stop when arriving at that destination. I am never content with the destination.

Being patient is about being resilient.

What do you do when progress slows down, gets complicated, and makes you question your direction?

There is a fine line between the adrenaline that propels success, the anxiety that sparks worry, and the anger that derails progress. The arousal driving all three processes pushes your internal systems to the brink, and the only thing controlling which way you go is your current perspective.

Engaging in a challenge and being patient at the outset is hard, and it is better to be a bit reckless than protective.

Go.

Adapt.

Continue forward.

Repeat.

You will encounter difficulties. You will see some coming and others arriving out of nowhere. You can navigate the challenges if you can be flexible, patient in your progress assessment, and resilient in your actions. If you get judgmental, angry, and frustrated that struggle has found you, your patience will drop, and you will panic, sparking much more anxiety.

You are built to handle more difficulties than you believe, and the only way to learn this is to develop the mental processes to accept uncertainty and find the power to push through the struggles. Experience is the most outstanding education you can have, but you must be willing to allow the learning to take hold.

Pushing forward despite the struggles creates patience because your focus is on progress, not a timeline.

Remember, you are a work in progress. If you assign your value to your outcomes, you will never achieve the validation you think you need. Focusing on the moment requires incredible patience, as you understand that you are the most stable aspect within the chaos of competition and uncertainty.

Just because things get difficult does not predict further challenges, and fear does not ever predict bad outcomes with 100% accuracy. Fear suggests that the probability of struggle is higher, like predicting thunderstorms in a weather forecast.

Your anxiety wants you to believe you are not good enough, it is not happening fast enough, and that others are better than you. It is time to be better than your fears.

Those negative voices in your head do not predict the future nor make conclusions about who you are as a person or player. Your anxiety is not defining you but reminding you that you have more to offer, can accept what is happening to you, and still proceed towards your goals despite all the internal noise in your head. That is the beauty of having a mindset to push through anxiety.

17

IT ALL COMES DOWN TO EMOTIONAL DISCIPLINE

My experiences with anxiety have never gone away. It is always there, sometimes running behind the scenes, destroying the foundations of my thoughts and beliefs.

At other times, it rages like a forest fire for the whole world to see.

Maybe the fact that my anxiety never goes away is the most frustrating experience with anxiety. That frustration fires up my anger, eventually resulting in more anxiety because I cannot control the pain arising from the anxiety.

You would think that something that could be so painful, that takes over your emotions and influences your actions, would be able to be controlled.

Something that controls you should be controlled, right? If you can find relief from numerous physical health conditions, like the flu, strep throat, or even vomiting, you *should* be able to stop the pain of anxiety.

And yet, here we are.

"Am I Out of Control?"

Over the last five years, anxiety has grown faster than the number of spots I have in my practice. I get flooded with calls, messages, and requests for help with anxiety. The requests all seem to start the same way – "I feel that I have lost my ability to control my thoughts, feel more stressed and anxious, and I cannot get a hold of it. I wasn't like this last year, but I cannot get it together now."

I have shared stages at national conferences with Olympic athletes who nearly lost their careers due to anxiety, had late-night phone calls with concerned parents about the welfare of their children, and talked coaches through their struggles while worried about the suffering of their athletes. Anxiety takes control and does not look for weakness; instead, it thrives over what you feel is your strength.

"I feel that I am losing my mind!"

"I know you are," I answer. "But the harder you try to gain control, the more you lose your emotional discipline, and anxiety thrives."

"Emotional discipline?

I am disciplined. I meditate, work out, and plan my days. How should I be disciplined if I cannot control my emotions?"

Stephen was an elite collegiate golfer on the trajectory of becoming a successful professional. Throughout his developmental years, he had been disciplined in his training, worked hard to separate himself from his competition, and always seemed to have the "It" factor. When he showed up to tournaments, there was an aura about him that highlighted that he was better than other players.

He could have been better, but he always found a way. He had earned All-American status throughout every level of golf, even in college. He earned opportunities to play in PGA Tour tournaments during college and always did well. He made a cut on the PGA Tour, had sponsors recruiting him, and was preparing for his professional career.

And then anxiety walked into his life.

The anxiety did not present as "yips," panic attacks, or even debilitating performance anxiety. Stephen did not struggle in the traditional ways, and the anxiety did not negatively affect his level of play. He was suffering in silence, eroding from the inside out.

When Stephen reached out, his mind was all over the place. His speech rate was hyper-speed, describing ten things in a space generally reserved for five. His focus was so distracted that he rarely finished one train of thought before getting distracted by three more.

The worst thing was that he was tough on himself.

His descriptions were very judgmental, layered with questions about his mental fortitude and strength, such as "What am I doing wrong that this would happen to me now?" While that question seems minimal, it is destructive.

Stephen had control of his game, life, and preparation for so long. He knew he was better than nearly every player in the field and believed he was one of the best players in the country. At tournaments, it didn't matter how he played because he would always grind through struggles to get into contention, finding a way to win. He loved winning and saw that mental acuity as his strength.

Yet, now he was struggling. No one on the outside knew it, could sense it, or even saw a decline in his performance. Instead, Stephen was destroying himself by judging the struggles as a sign of something wrong.

He would sit in his room at night and analyze every aspect of his game. His focus shifted to fixing the discomfort, and he became terrified of turning professional, only to potentially fail and be exposed as a fraud. He thought he could diagnose the problem, fix it, and continue as if nothing had ever happened, especially hiding it from everyone else.

"Doc, in a tournament now, when I have to grind with my C-level game, that pisses me off. Why do I have to do that? If I want to succeed as a professional, that cannot happen. I have to have my A-game, or I will have to find a job fast."

"How often do you have your C-game or worse?" I asked.

"Seems like all the time. I used to be able to find my A-game, and it was so easy when it was there. You must realize that my A-game is there when I practice, and I can play better if I have it more."

"So, describe what happens when you don't have your A-game?"

"I get frustrated because I have put in so much work. I can do it in practice with the guys on the team and even in money matches. I work harder than everyone else and love this game so much. Honestly, I hate how it makes me feel, and I don't want to have this as a career if my life is miserable. It shouldn't be this hard. Look at my past, as I never really struggled, or if I did, I could overcome it – quickly. I was the best at that!"

"Wait, there is a lot there. Let's return to your feelings when you do not have your A-game. Tell me what you feel is off."

The difference between your best and your average is often the most critical distinction that demonstrates the lack of discipline in the emotional side of the game. Stephen's description started with the fact that something was off in his game and then quickly cascaded to judgment, fear of the future, and lack of belief in himself. When Stephen latched on to "I used to be able to," this highlights a lack of belief in the present moment because he romanticizes the past and fears the future. It is an important distinction.

Players rarely have their A-game. It does not matter the sport, competitive environment, or circumstance. You have your A-game about 5-10% of the time and play your way into it instead of creating it. I want my professional golfers to believe so much in their ability to play with their B-minus, C-plus game that they can contend in any tournament.

That trust in their suboptimal game requires enhancing awareness of how they play with those levels, what they feel, and most importantly, where their mind goes when they don't have the A-game. Most undisciplined emotionally start judging, questioning, panicking, and searching. My players accept, stay present, and grind.

I had to shift Stephen's thinking that he did not need to be perfect to compete. When struggle showed up, Stephen chased the discomfort to find relief, not believing he could beat the field with his C-game, biding time until the A-game appeared—searching instead of staying present.

The Difference Between Emotional Discipline and Being Undisciplined

Stephen was spinning himself into misery, searching for relief from his anxieties. At the core of his anxiety was the fear of the future and uncertainty about succeeding as a professional golfer.

Due to that fear, he was highly critical of his level of play, used every day as a measuring stick for the future, and was so hard on himself that he could not see progress, only continuous evidence of his deficiencies.

He had found himself undisciplined, a captive to his emotions and a prisoner to his anxiety.

Emotionally undisciplined players impulsively react to every discomfort and actively search for relief, not growth. That urgency to fix gets magnified by concern over their future and the potential that things will worsen. The earliest signals of discomfort trigger a cascade of threat-based thoughts, an increased need to control nearly every aspect of their performance, and the focus to avert struggle instead of learning to play through it.

Undisciplined players find themselves thinking so fast in competition, chasing the fixes to their problems, and before they realize it, they have lost chunks of time in games. Being undisciplined has you chasing, not competing.

Stephen had stopped grinding because he was trying to measure against a mythical performance standard, even if it was not objective. As a result, every competitive event became a need to validate he was good enough, not a learning laboratory to improve. The more he "needed," the further he was away from his true competitive self.

After competitions, Stephen would experience significant levels of frustration and regret. He was piling on the negative assessments and destroying his self-image to try to improve. The only hope for a positive future is if he proves he was good enough today.

I needed him to embrace emotional discipline. Not controlling the internal or external world, but shifting his perspective, growing his ability to endure, and learning to develop his C-plus/B-minus game.

Emotionally disciplined individuals learn to accept their present circumstances or level of play as simply the experience of the moment, not a test of their worth or validation of their ability. Instead of reacting to every struggle, chasing fixes, and fighting to escape the pain, emotionally disciplined athletes challenge themselves to learn something at the moment to build a better future. The mental shift is a change of perspective, away from judgment and into wisdom growing.

The term "discipline" is not a challenge of your strength but a reminder to shift your focus to a more effective process. Your mental state creates your outcomes and circumstances when discipline is high. When low, your circumstances are in charge of your perspective. Discipline is more about the level of influence.

EMOTIONALLY UNDISCIPLINED

EVENTS DETERMINE EMOTIONS WITHOUT LOGIC

DECISIONS ARE INFLUENCED BY EMOTION

RESULTS DETERMINE STATE OF MIND

LEVELS OF EMOTION CREATE NEGATIVE IMPACT

PREVENTION > PURPOSE

INFLUENCED BY SELF IMAGE, WORK INVESTED, TRUST IN FUTURE

EMOTIONALLY FLEXIBLE

EVENTS DO NOT CREATE STATE OF MIND

YOUR STATE OF MIND RISES ABOVE EMOTIONS

RESET INTO NEXT MOMENT WITHOUT CARRYOVER

Throughout this book, I have provided the different tools to take control of your anxiety, and there is no greater "control" than being disciplined. Anxiety in life or performance settings will only control you if you give up your emotional power to chase quick fixes, relief, or comfort.

Being emotionally undisciplined assumes you are broken and need fixing; there is no evidence. You may suffer, struggle, and not do great, but you are not broken. You need to build your support systems – internally by how you think and externally by those who help you.

Emotionally disciplined individuals experience discomfort and anxiety but direct their energy towards enduring the suffering. Anxiety does not go away; it quiets down for periods and comes back in others, but when you are disciplined, you are prepared. When undisciplined, you react to every warning sign as if it predicts your ultimate demise.

To become emotionally disciplined, here are a few steps that may help.

1. Reframe your First Reaction:

Struggle will happen, so instead of reacting to your feelings, try to see the challenge from a different perspective. Your response takes tremendous acceptance that you are okay in the emotional storm. You do not need to fix your discomfort.

For Stephen, the most critical shift was changing his initial reaction to try to predict his future. I had him understand that struggle was the standard, not the exception. Given that fact, I wanted him to invite struggles in to learn to become a better player in those moments.

2. Direct Your Focus to the Next Action:

When anxiety or struggle builds, your mind processes information rapidly. Your mind searches for the next threat and scans for the escape route. As a result, your actions tend to be very reactionary and not the most productive. Instead, ask yourself, "What can I do to progress?" The "little bit" is crucial because you tell yourself you are okay at that moment but want to move forward.

For Stephen, this was about determining what the next shot would be. When his anxiety started to build in the past, his mind cascaded into preventing bad shots, protecting against mistakes, and trying to control the outcome. By shifting into "the little bit," he could focus on the plan of a shot he wanted to hit. The mental storm could slow down and not hijack his emotions.

3. Change your Evaluation Metrics:

When your anxiety rises, your mind has one goal – relief from the pain and discomfort. The outcome becomes complete relief or total failure, an all-or-nothing perspective impossible to attain. Ask yourself, "What can I learn?" instead. Wisdom requires exposure to uncomfortable scenarios, and your anxiety reflects that discomfort. Use those moments to learn about your emotional resolve, challenging situations, and thoughts or feelings.

For Stephen, I had him become an "interested observer" in those stressful or high-anxiety moments and journal the experiences. By turning himself into an interested observer, he stopped reacting to every feeling or thought. It was a powerful perspective shift!

4. Accept What You Can Do:

Finally, realize that you still have the power to do something productive in every challenging circumstance. You are not paralyzed by anxiety, crushed by fear, and imprisoned from progressing despite what your mind tells you. You can do something productive, even if one of those "little bits."

For Stephen, we developed the C-game strategy that empowered him to have something he could trust when his mind was rushing, his heart was pounding, and he was highly judgmental. This strategy gave him a safety net that he could do something and was not powerless. When he was in the throes of being undisciplined emotionally, he spent his energy on everything but what he could do. Now, he started to see that his "C-game strategy" started beating his other competitors, showing progress.

When anxiety ramps up, have a plan for a productive perspective shift instead of reacting to the discomfort with protective or fear-driven actions. The more you can learn your capability to endure uncertainty and discomfort, the more power you gain to direct your focus to factors that matter. As a result, your mental state changes your perception of your circumstances, not vice versa.

This mental redirection is a massive shift that is needed for you to take power back from your anxiety. Emotional discipline gives you the ability to progress instead of protect. The presence of discomfort or struggle is nothing more than an invitation to get better in those moments, not predicting a more challenging future. The more you protect because of being undisciplined emotionally, the more you collapse into your own space. You will grow if you can find the discipline to direct your focus on your progress.

Growth is the antidote for anxiety and the only thing that turns the volume down on the pain and suffering. But with growth comes more uncertainty, so you must stay disciplined in every circumstance, internally and externally.

As he prepared for his professional career, Stephen embraced the challenge of learning to become more emotionally disciplined. Instead of chasing the fixes or believing that he was a broken human being, he turned the anxiety into fuel to learn more about himself and as a catalyst to develop "professional" skill sets. When he started to experience increased anxiety, he used the discomfort as a catalyst to direct his focus on learning about the moment and the challenges he was facing.

If he had a tough day, he explored the experience instead of chasing the "why." There was no "why" to understand. Discomfort, anxiety, and struggle happened, and he began to realize that he could not control the occurrence but could shift his perspective toward his ability within the experience.

Your power to direct your focus is your embodiment of discipline. Stephen started learning in every challenging experience, leading him to the PGA Tour, where he has won several times. To this day, he texts me when circumstances get difficult to share what he learned.

His wisdom is his superpower!

Anxiety can only control you when you lose your discipline. To defeat anxiety, beat its influence on you.

The anxiety I experience will never disappear; I know and have learned to accept it. When I realized that I could direct my focus to what I wanted despite what or how I felt, I gained control over my anxiety.

Does anxiety still hurt? Yes.

Does my anxiety still show up when I do not want it? Absolutely.

Have I had another experience on an airplane? Yes, while writing this book. Did I vomit? I wanted to, but as I was sitting in my seat, I created a plan should I get sick on the plane. Those contingency plans gave me power and allowed me to be disciplined despite my feelings. Instead of feeling relief when it was over, I felt empowered to take on the next challenge.

What did I learn?

My mind amplifies the situation when I feel unprepared to progress. When I have a plan, I can manage my mind and progress in the chaos of any situation.

Did this happen? Of course. This most recent experience occurred on a flight to Maui for the Tournament of Champions for the PGA Tour. As I was sitting on the flight to Maui, the stomach bug that I had been fighting for a few days gurgled up. For five hours, I battled my stomach, nausea, and anxiety. I was sweating and squirming in my seat. I sat in my seat and developed a plan should I need to vomit. I never did, thankfully.

When the plane landed, I shifted my mind away from relief and immediately asked myself what I had learned. The revelation was this – "I can face anything if I embrace the discomfort and push forward."

When we got to the hotel, my oldest daughter asked me to do a SCUBA lesson. SCUBA diving was not anywhere on my bucket list. My initial reaction was to decline, but instead, I told her to book the lesson. I wanted to immerse myself in misery again, and I *needed* to do it.

As the lesson started, I began to experience intense anxiety, especially when breathing underwater. Since we started in the pool, it was easy to stand up, but my mind kept shifting to "What are you going to do in the ocean?"

I faced that question by saying, "What do I need to do to breathe better right here?" The dive master gave me a short breathing trick, and I found my emotional discipline. I tried to get anxious underwater to test the breathing plan and navigated through the discomfort every time.

While walking to the ocean, I developed a plan if my anxiety spiked underwater in the ocean, 200 yards away from the shore. I could feel my heart rate increasing, but I worked the plan to perfection instead!

SCUBA was incredible. Not just because of the views but the experience of facing something that sparked my anxiety, and I developed the discipline to meet it. We have already planned to do it again. Why? Because I must practice what I preach, and I need to be emotionally disciplined to face the things that spike my anxiety.

The only way I can learn to beat anxiety is to beat the shit out of it – by being disciplined despite what I think, feel, or experience. Anxiety has no power over me when I have the plan to flow with it.

18

THE PATHWAY TO WINNING

I love the smell of French fries from McDonald's. There is something special about the crispy, salty shoestring potatoes that hit differently than other fast-food brands.

Those French fries do not smell right when you are fighting anxiety attacks that trigger painful nausea. Not much in McDonald's does at that moment.

To understand the pathway to help you Kick Anxiety's Ass, I need to take you back to my misery during graduate school. It is essential to understand that the anxiety or panic attacks I was having back in graduate school seemed to come out of the blue, but the reality was that I had always struggled with anxiety. I "ran hot."

Anxiety is part of my psychological fingerprint. I dealt with it, found ways to compete with it, and never seemed bothered by it growing up. I thought it was normal. Back then, I thought normal would be calm, peaceful, and no anxiety. Now, I appreciate that normal is anxious as hell.

When the panic attacks started, I could not sit there and allow them to beat me. I had to fight them and find a way that worked for me. I found myself dreading social situations, didn't want to get on a flight, and would skip my graduate school classes.

Anxiety started to beat me down. I was losing my confidence, and that scared me.

I was not going to let anxiety win. I was ready to enter the ring to fight anxiety, but because I had never liked to lose, I had to find a way to destroy anxiety.

First, I had to accept that my anxiety was spiking at that moment. I had a lot going on and had to stop asking "why" and start asking "what." I had to let go of "why this was happening to me," and I asked, "What did the anxiety feel like, and what was triggering it?"

That was a decisive step toward acceptance, an essential step in gaining perspective. Anxiety clouds your perspective, so anything I could do to appreciate the influence of anxiety in my life was critical. I also planned to face it head-on, where I feared anxiety the most – in a crowded restaurant.

I told myself I would vomit in the restaurant but that my misery would not embarrass me but make me better. Another step of perspective sparked a reframing of something painful in me. The physical perception of my panic attacks was not saying my anxiety was winning, but rather that I would learn what I felt and how those feelings made me feel.

If anxiety is nothing but arousal and energy, I would not fight against it anymore but instead use that energy towards a goal. I wanted to be comfortable again.

I set a plan in motion. I would eat lunch daily at McDonald's on campus and learn to eat in public again. I accepted that my anxiety would be high, but I would start to pay attention to what my body and mind were projecting, even if it were vomit. I would listen to the storm in my head as if trying to record the experiences.

I would order an entire lunch consisting of a Big Mac, large French fries, and a large Diet Coke, as my goal was not to cut any corners. I would eat the entire lunch and then sit.

And suffer.

And fight nausea.

And look for an escape route.

And plan for the moment that the vomit started its ejection procedures.

My goal was to sit there for 10 minutes.

It was brutal. I dreaded lunch, feared the moment, and prayed that every day for lunch, there would be an open table by the door or bathroom.

But every moment the clock moved another minute, I beat anxiety. I anchored myself on two things –

> · I wanted to feel the seat against my back, providing a solid grounding so when my head started spinning, I would feel the chair against my back
>
> · I had never vomited in public, despite all the anxiety that I had been experiencing. The truth was that my fears were creating a story that did not exist.

It is rational to know that I had never actually vomited, but the irrational part of my mind suggested that I would vomit the next time I was in a surge of anxiety. The potential was worse than reality, and I had to anchor myself back into reality.

After a week of eating in that McDonald's for 10 minutes, it had stretched to 45 minutes, and then eventually, I could leave when I wanted. At first, I experienced relief when I left. After a week, I felt accomplished.

I was not going to fight the feelings anymore. The panic attacks taught me that both the sudden surges of anxiety and generalized anxiety would be a part of my life, but I would face them instead of blocking them.

I had learned to change my perspective toward my anxiety. I no longer saw it as a negative influence on me but maybe something that helped me connect to people. My worries and fears were not always rational, but they inspired me to prepare for every scenario with the fullest intentions and not to stop.

I learned to meditate, focus on breathing, and exercise when stressed. I had associated the slightest perception of anxiety as unfavorable, but I wanted to use the energy that came with anxiety. There is power in positive energy and destruction in negative, reactive energy. I wanted the positive benefits.

To beat anxiety, I wanted to use it. Instead of being confused that my anxiety was spiking in a social situation or worried about a client, I developed a small strategy to face the anxiety, redirect my fears, and be aggressive toward something meaningful. I am not perfect in this and still experience significant anxiety, but I have a grounding that I can return to when I need it. This approach works nearly every time I use it. Unfortunately, I forget about it—just the truth.

The Five A's

Taking action amid anxiety risks reactivity. You lose your discipline to act purposefully, chasing the drama of fighting fears and avoiding pain. The five A's help me see anxiety with a purpose, not just reacting to the misery of the moment.

When you feel your anxiety, think about these five A's, and you will push through and, in doing so, start kicking anxiety's ass.

1. Acceptance

"What is happening to you has already happened, and trying to prevent it only worsens the experience."

"Nothing is happening to you right now that you cannot respond to."

Those two mindset shifts reframed the way I viewed my anxiety.

For far too long, I worked to prevent the negative feelings of anxiety.

I hated how it made me feel and felt that I was less than adequate simply because I was suffering from anxiety.

Yet, there was nothing I could do about it. I am an anxious person and have been my whole life. Even training to become a clinical psychologist, I listened to lecture after lecture about taking the negative experiences of anxiety and fighting to replace them with constructive or calming thoughts. That cannot happen.

I had to start accepting who I was and what I was experiencing. If I could focus on accepting the energy and power of anxiety, could I become better and manage my world around it?

My anxiety does not, did not, and will not define who I am. I have anxiety, but I am not *anxiety*. A powerful perspective starts with awareness and acceptance of what is happening and who you are.

Once I realized I had greater power over what I felt, I could accept my feelings, anxieties, and challenges. Acceptance gave me tremendous power to be productive and abandon the need to protect.

Think about it, like the weather and climate. I grew up in south Louisiana, a hot and humid environment that could be quite oppressive in the summer. Regular days would have over 90-degree heat, around 90-degree humidity, and a 90 percent chance of thunderstorms in the early afternoon.

It would rain "somewhere" during the summer more days than not. It may not rain in your location, but somewhere over the region, there was a high likelihood that it was storming for 45 minutes.

Knowing the climate makes you realize that thunderstorms are just part of the experience and are minute-by-minute weather. Even on days with hurricanes, you knew that the weather that day was a mere expression of the climate but did not define the more extensive understanding of the climate.

The climate is your overall mental framework.

The weather is your moment-by-moment experience.

I learned to separate my weather from the definition of my climate. I could be doing great things and seeing great success but experience some anxiety, which is fair and possible. The feelings at the moment, however, did not define my worth.

Feeling anxious right now did not mean I would have a bad day.

Feeling tense did not mean something wrong was going to happen.

I just accepted what I felt as a moment-by-moment experience.

Acceptance.

No judgment. No fortune-telling. No predicting the future.

To manage the feelings you experience, you must first accept their presence. You did not choose to have them, are not wrong for having them, or are less an effective competitor because you have them. They are there, and how you deal with them matters the most.

Think about having a panic attack. The feelings are scary, and your mind goes to some crazy places. How effective have you been fighting the feelings or preventing them from happening?

The more you resist them, the more power you give them, and the stronger they become. You are feeding what you fear.

2. Anchoring

If you cannot change your experience, you must find stability in your mindset. Stability in this framework is like planting your feet solidly on the ground.

I use videos every day in my sessions with my athletes. I do so because I can find different perspectives across different environments that may connect to a particular athlete. There is one video I use more than any other.

Destin Sandin is an engineer turned vlogger in north Alabama. As a former Missile Flight Test Engineer at the Redstone Arsenal, a US Army post that collaborates with NASA and other military contractors for weapon and missile development, Sandin began vlogging topics he found intriguing, documenting his educational journey.

His vlogs transformed into *Smarter Every Day* in 2011 and have nearly 11 million subscribers on YouTube. Each video explores scientific phenomena across sports, the military, and technology.

In Episode 201, <u>Strapped into a Sinking Helicopter (with U.S. Marines)</u>, Sandin visited the Advanced Helo Underwater Egress Training at Marine Corps Base Hawaii, where he trained with Marines in the event of an underwater emergency when aboard a helicopter. While training aboard a helicopter, Marines were submerged in a pool and provided with the strategy to escape safely.

As the helicopter begins to submerge, the apparent thought would be to unbuckle as soon as possible and find the nearest opening to escape. The Marine instructors demonstrate why this is the worst possible decision during the training. Why?

Simple – when you are in a hurry to escape the sinking helicopter, you abandon all the anchors that will help you survive. In a rush to survive, you will lose your bearings, dump your oxygen tanks, and panic. Instead, they train Marines to stay anchored.

Specifically, instructors trained the Marines to grasp their seats like a cowboy holding onto their saddles, sitting firmly in their seats to gather their bearings, in which they could then grab their oxygen and breathe safely. The Marines can get enough oxygen and find a safe exit by slowing down and staying anchored.

This video has over 20 million views on YouTube, and I bet I recommended a quarter of them!

Why? Because the anchoring technique is a brilliant example of what to do when experiencing a flood of anxiety.

The natural tendency is to escape the threatening environment and protect yourself from what you feel. The problem is your mind switches to protection and away from purpose. The more you try to protect yourself from your anxiety and the threatening environment, the worse decisions you make.

Instead, could you find your anchor in life? It could be three deep diaphragmatic breaths, a prayer you recite, squeezing your hands together, and releasing. Regardless of what it is, your anchor provides a stable process to rely on despite the drama around you.

I had to find my anchor. When my anxiety peaked in the past, I often found myself all over the place mentally. I would center on the worries I would let people down or fail to commit. Those worries just led me into a negative cycle. Finding an anchor gave me stability in the center of the storm.

My anchor was my breathing. I have been a fan of breathing-based meditation or relaxation ever since I was in college. I have found that I hold my anxiety mostly in my chest or tight in my shoulders, leading to headaches or difficulty breathing.

Maybe it is because I was diagnosed with asthma later in life that I would have trouble breathing when I was younger, but breathing gives me stability.

I do not expect my anxiety to decrease when I do my breathing exercises. Instead, I breathe to ride with the anxiety and focus on describing my feelings. If I start to wander mentally, locking into different anxieties, I return to the depth of the breath that I am taking in.

I have started to extend this breathing practice to times when I do not have significant anxiety. Mornings can be challenging because I get worked up over the responsibilities on my To-Do lists. I may have 15 clients on my calendar, and I have five phone calls with Tour players, two chapters I need to finish writing, and answer calls from coaches. Knowing my day will be a proverbial fire drill can work me up. As a result, I started doing some breathing and mental awareness every morning at my desk.

I needed to start working on my breathing exercises in the exact place where I experienced the most significant angst. Instead of rushing through the 15 minutes before my day starts, I feel the experiences associated with my breathing. Just being present with my breathing has helped me stay anchored and not get in a hurry to mess more things up.

I still have anxiety. Twenty-five years after my first panic attack, I still worry that I will have more sudden attacks, particularly on airplanes.

That will never go away, but I feel more grounded when experiencing an overwhelming storm of anxiety.

Find something that you can do to be your anchor. Thoughts and "staying positive" cannot hold up against the cascade of psychological and physiological arousal—the more physical the activity, the better.

Try the following:

· Rub your hands together and focus your mind on the sensation of your hands, even if they are sweaty, cold, or clammy

· Yoga poses and stretches can be very beneficial, although they can be hard to do discretely

· Recite a prayer and song lyric

· Counting can work, too.

Anxiety is the comprehensive hijacking of the physiological and psychological systems, so you must have an anchor to provide tangible stability so the noise, urgency, and arousal can pass.

3. Action

Your thoughts lead to feelings, which leads to action. The Cognitive Triangle is a long-standing psychological perspective but gets overlooked in favor of more complex answers. Yet, its genius is its simplicity.

All action is created by a thought process, sparking a feeling that fuels the action. Central to the foundations of the cognitive-behavioral therapy approach, thoughts, feelings, and actions are interrelated.

Since thoughts rise from below your conscious awareness, they drive feelings. Feelings are the emotional experience of a group of thoughts and consistent themes. For instance, you could have thoughts of "I am struggling. I am not good enough. I will never succeed." Those repetitive thoughts may lead to a feeling of despair.

How would despair impact the action you take?

That is crucial because we cannot change our thoughts. Your actions are often automatic, quickly taken, and motivated by emotion.

Sometimes, that is beneficial, especially when you do not have the time to evaluate every possibility. Negative emotions and feelings fuel impulsive actions and result in less-than-ideal outcomes.

To succeed in the face of anxiety, you must learn to take appropriate action, not be driven by the impulsive need to escape discomfort, and not overanalyze for fear of making a mistake. Learn to take purposeful action; in doing so, you shift the cognitive triangle away from the downward destruction of cascading negativity towards positive action. This type of action prepares you to adapt to your surroundings instead of being stuck in repetitive negative patterns.

Anxiety wants you to protect, to take any action that prevents an outcome instead of doing something with purpose and intention. You must act on what you want and not give in to drama inside your mind.

Acting with intention is so tricky. Anxiety tells you why you should protect and proceed cautiously.

Yet, proceeding in competition and life by protecting against negative consequences ensures you will have less than desired outcomes. You may not suffer the pain you were protecting against, but you never succeeded. Face the fact that you cannot prevent failure and succeed with the same intention. Those are two different objectives.

When anxiety spikes, golfers try to avoid hitting a terrible shot, protecting against missing the ball in the worst part of the hole. Without fail, they struggle to hit great shots.

Baseball pitchers who are afraid to walk hitters spend their time on the mound lacking the direction and command to dominate hitters.

People who try to prevent the occurrence of a panic attack only raise their arousal so high that an anxiety attack is always on the brink.

It is simple to observe from the outside but brutal to experience when anxiety dominates your thought processes.

Your action must focus on what you want to accomplish despite your feelings or worries.

4. Adaptation

"Why did you shake me off?" Coach Bertman asked me. It was the bottom of the fifth inning in my first collegiate start against the University of South Alabama.

I never liked being a starting pitcher. I remember the anxiety associated with starting a baseball game as early as third grade, and I would dread the game if I knew I would start that day.

I loved the adrenaline of being a relief pitcher and rising to the occasion of the troublesome moment in a game. The job from the bullpen was addictive to me, but starting a game led me to have painful doubts and crippling anxiety.

As my junior season progressed, I pitched in every situation possible at LSU. I led the team in appearances and contributed to a successful season while accumulating solid pitching statistics. After a conference weekend, Coach Bertman asked me to start the midweek game to prepare for the postseason. When he told me that I would start, my stomach dropped.

For the three-day lead-up, I dreaded the start. I couldn't sleep, and I struggled to keep my mind on positive themes.

To give context, the University of South Alabama was an excellent baseball school. The team that year boasted several players who would play in Major League Baseball, perennially in the postseason. This game was not a patsy, and I had to be on my game.

I managed the early struggles of the game reasonably well, but I found myself in trouble in the top of the fifth inning. I had gotten the bases loaded and was struggling with command. I had no problem pitching six or seven innings, but I knew I had to complete the fifth inning to earn the victory. We were up three runs, and if I got taken out of the game before the top of the fifth inning was over, someone else would get the victory. Hey, that is what starting pitchers think about – victories.

With three balls and two strikes count with two outs, I had to make the pitch. I knew the reliever was ready in the bullpen, and if I did not get this hitter out, this might be my last pitch.

The catcher signaled for a fastball on the outer third of the plate.

I shook it off.

Typically, a fastball is the most straightforward pitch to throw for a pitcher. Also, with a full count with two outs and the bases loaded, the hitter will be looking for a fastball. Everyone in the stands knows that, too. As a pitcher, your back is not just against the wall but getting buried by that wall.

The catcher signaled for a slider on the outside part of the plate.

I nodded yes.

I threw the slider, the hitter swung and missed, and I got the strikeout, finished the inning, and stayed in the game.

Coach Bertman approached me as I ran off the field and asked why I shook him off. At LSU, Coach Bertman called every single pitch of the game. He was a genius at calling pitches and had so much knowledge of the opponent and pitchers that it was easier to follow his lead.

Coach spent considerable time training the pitchers because he felt they were an extension of him on the field. I sat through hours of classroom meetings every year, learning the game from the inside out.

"Coach, when I lose my release point, a slider helps me pitch more aggressively," was my answer to Coach's question.

"Got it. Thanks!" Coach replied.

I was not avoiding the fastball, but at that moment, with what I was feeling, I wanted the slider. I trusted the slider at that moment.

He did not care if a pitcher shook him off in a game, but he just wanted to understand why to be more efficient later.

Coach wanted us prepared, but he valued our ability to adapt. To pitch for Coach, you had to demonstrate that you could self-correct your mechanics, manage the difficulties of a high-pressure game, and withstand surges from your opponent. If you could not adapt to the moment's heat, you would not play at LSU.

Coach used to tell us that if we needed an invitation to adapt, then the game would bypass us. That advice is also accurate for dealing with anxiety in the heat of any moment.

You have an elite mental skill that you often overlook: your ability to adapt to a changing environment. That does not mean you are changing, abandoning, or retreating.

Adaptability means making small mental pivots in the face of challenges that spark changes toward success.

Your ability to adapt will increase your probability of succeeding. Just like the muscles in your body must be flexible to endure the demands placed on them, your mind must also be flexible to survive any challenge.

Adapting to anxiety is finding one step forward when your mind tells you to stop or retreat. It is a simple shift to see what is possible, moving away from what is painful.

Negative thoughts want you to believe you cannot progress, but what is that hard with a simple adjustment pushing forward?

Can you adjust your vision to just being better in the heat of the moment?

Can you let go of the fear of anxiety and the associated drama it brings and instead see your struggle differently?

Can you express just a little gratitude for what you are going through?

5. Analysis

When your life ends, your life learnings represent wisdom on a bookshelf. What type of books and lessons will be on your bookshelf?

By the presence of anxiety in your life, you could assume that you get exposed to significant uncertainty across difficult circumstances. If that is the case, those new environments have served as tremendous learning environments. The question is, what are you doing with those learnings?

I find too many focus on escaping and surviving challenging environments and, when it is over, move on quickly, hoping never to experience them again. The fear of "what if" inspires much more action than the desire to achieve, and this happens because the pain of struggle persists longer than the joy of success.

Learn, or you will repeat the difficulties.

Taking time to review experiences is a powerful tool for engaging in learning. Whether journaling, post-competition statistical review, or summary reports, there must be a framework to download the mental information encountered during complex, challenging, or adrenaline-spiking moments.

How much can you remember if you sit in class and do not take notes?

Sitting back and villainizing every decision you make throughout the day is easy.

Why did I do that?

What was I thinking?

What did I do wrong?

That line of questioning is not constructive, even though it is natural to reflect critically. When you are critical in your analysis, you assume that your level of performance or even progress is excellent until you make mistakes.

It is a top-down approach like everything is great until I make mistakes, which detracts from what I do. Instead, start to see things from a bottom-up approach, starting at zero and building performance and success.

When you analyze, look at what triggers an increase in anxiety, not from the perspective of disappointment, anger, and frustration, but what factors sparked the increased arousal. Further, what was the theme of your thoughts when the anxiety intensified?

Did they funnel back into a consistent theme of a threat or insecurity? Those moments are critical for growth and learning.

Examining themes, particularly those that reflect insecurities, provides a learning laboratory to challenge them. For instance, if the increased anxiety in competition led to negative thoughts of:

"Why do I always struggle here?"

"Everyone will see me as a failure!

No one else seems to fail. I must get through this because everyone will realize that I am not that good if I struggle!"

Thoughts like that are common and meaningless unless attached to insecurity, such as "I don't think I am good enough to be here."

Imposter syndrome is prevalent among competitors. Even if you doubt you are good enough to be in your position, you can still succeed.

Imposter syndrome motivates you to work harder, prepare more, and lower your expectations. There is a purpose behind those doubts.

Learn to become one of the best in the world instead of fearing that you will not live up to someone else's expectations. Face those doubts and turn them into determination.

No one will cure anxiety. You cannot get rid of an underlying physiological system designed to help you simply because it is uncomfortable.

You can learn to live with anxiety and thrive. Your view of your anxiety is critical because you cannot develop a plan to function with it if you are running from discomfort. Yes, it hurts and can hijack every part of you, but you are not at risk of losing to anxiety. That can only happen if you react to the anxiety and lose faith in your ability to push through.

19

ANXIETY IS NOT A LIFE SENTENCE

Anxiety only controls those who give up power to the pain of anxiety. I know it hurts and suggests your future will be formidable. Anxiety tells lies and robs you of your power to persevere.

But it does not have to.

If you are struggling with anxiety, having doubts about your performance, or questioning if you can succeed, you can succeed if you are willing to face the doubts, insecurities, and discomfort in your life. Whatever happens to you or despite your feelings, you can find the strength to push forward with growth, development, and learning.

The rates of anxiety are exploding across the country, particularly in our younger generations. Athletes are self-reporting anxiety at alarming rates as well.

There are many reasons for this anxiety growth, particularly among athletes, but the causes are not as important to me as the solutions. Societal factors, the reliance upon social media, and the need for earlier athletic success drive so much pain. Still, we lack the tools to face the anxiety individually and as institutions. It is time to address anxiety head-on.

The Short Circuit Society

The performance matrices across all aspects of life drive the need for quicker investment returns. If you're struggling to pay attention, find a Doctor Who can prescribe you Adderall. If you're unhappy, find somebody to prescribe you medication that makes you less unhappy. But the one thing that we need help with is that we don't see growth as the standard.

Instead, we seek relief. When we have built a world of finding solace, it leads us to drown in an endless cycle of despair. The feeling of relief is the absence of something painful, and the feeling of accomplishment is achieving something difficult.

Too many of us work for relief, and we feel the uncomfortable pain we're having due to anxiety and search for solutions that provide immediate relief. Instead, we must empower to endure, not strengthen the escape.

The anxiety you feel in every realm of your life identifies a problem. Instead, I want you to start seeing it as an invitation to face the anxiety, to work through the pain, to push into it with emotional discipline, and to learn more about yourself through it. Remember, your psychological fingerprint and its expression influence your philosophy, plan of attack and process. Take every uncomfortable situation and use it better for the next time.

You can only defeat anxiety by cutting off its energy source. When your anxiety dictates your reaction, it is in control, robbing your energy. You take control when you have a plan, are aware of your feelings, and can progress with whatever you are feeling. It is as simple as that.

This book helps you shift your power into elements you control. I want you to use your circumstances in your life to develop more powerful mental strategies, so every future challenge becomes a training ground versus a proving ground.

Anxiety will never go away, but your power to perform will increase. That is my goal.

It is only possible to prepare a warrior for battle if they can handle the changing demands of the challenge. The best warriors face the challenges with the attitude that they are the difference makers and can face anything because they are prepared to use their weapons against any unknown threat. Ultimately, the warrior and not the weapons determine the outcome.

For anxiety, it is not the techniques that matter but the belief you can handle any threat, respond to every challenge, and accept you can endure any discomfort. Once you believe that anxiety cannot defeat you, you will regain your power over anxiety.

In Closing

I hope this book provides some perspective, help you see things differently, and allows you to face life's challenges *with* anxiety head-on.

Anxiety is not a life sentence. It may feel like a prison, but it is far from it.

You cannot control many things in life, but you can control your focus. You can shift your perspective to view your experiences with anxiety differently. Instead of allowing your anxiety to burn throughout your life without guidance, you can direct it. You can manage it by understanding your relationship with anxiety.

It is time to show anxiety that it no longer controls you. You are more than your worst days, more powerful than your greatest insecurities, and stronger than your biggest fears.

Now is the time to face each fear, each moment of indecision, each gurgle in your stomach, and stress with the power to redirect that energy into productivity.

The dangers of today only exist in your mind of tomorrow. Your ability to face the immediate moments of your life is your power. Take that power forward.

ABOUT THE AUTHOR

Dr. Bhrett McCabe is the founder of The MindSide, a center for Sports and Performance Psychology, and trusted advisor for the top performing competitors in the country. Dr. McCabe combines his personal experience as a 2x National Champion Division I athlete, his training as a licensed clinical psychologist, and his corporate leadership experience to help competitors achieve an elite performance mindset. Dr. McCabe develops personalized strategies and processes to help athletes and businesses achieve success at the highest levels. Dr. McCabe serves as the Sports & Performance Psychologist for elite-level athletes, corporate leaders, and teams including The University of Alabama Athletics, PGA Tour, NFL, and NBA. Dr. McCabe's strategies are also trusted by high-achieving businesses including multiple Fortune 500 organizations, Andrews Sports Medicine, and Titleist Performance Institute.

Dr. McCabe is the author of *Break Free From Suckville*, which he has developed to help athletes and competitors in all arenas break free from the struggles they're in. Dr. McCabe also hosts a weekly live show on YouTube, Mental Game LIVE, and has published several academic journal articles, presented numerous scientific presentations, as well as provided insight and authored articles for trade magazines such as GOLF Magazine, Golf World, Golf Week, and ESPNW, among others. Dr. McCabe has made several appearances on The Golf Channel's Morning Drive and The Golf Fix.

WHAT'S NEXT?

If you do not subscribe or watch already, check out Dr. McCabe's weekly, LIVE YouTube show, **Mental Game LIVE**. Each episode, Dr. McCabe breaks down different topics involving mental performance so that you can take that knowledge and implement into your game! He also brings on elite athletes, coaches, and performers to discuss their take on mental performance and how they perform at the highest levels. Dr. McCabe also has a live Q & A every episode so you can get all of your mental game questions answered! Subscribe to his YouTube channel right now so you don't miss any of the action!

SUBSCRIBE: YouTube.com/@DrBhrettMcCabe

If you are more of a visual person, Dr. McCabe's virtual training courses provide in-depth, game-changing strategies to improve your outcomes in whichever competitive arena you wish to excel.

bhrettmccabe.com/virtual-training

FOLLOW DR. McCABE ON SOCIAL MEDIA

@DRBHRETTMCCABE

Made in United States
Troutdale, OR
09/05/2024

22615785R00137